The Lost Symbol Found

Unauthorized Analysis and Critique of Dan Brown's Latest Novel

Dr. Graeme Davis

NIMBLE BOOKS LLC

Nimble Books LLC

1521 Martha Avenue

Ann Arbor, MI, USA 48103

http://www.NimbleBooks.com

wfz@nimblebooks.com

+1.734-330-2593

Version 1.0; last saved 2009-11-15.

Printed in the United States of America

ISBN-13: 978-1-608880-119

♾ The paper used in this publication meets the minimum requirements of the American National Standard for Information Sciences—Permanence of Paper for Printed Library Materials, ANSI Z39.48-1992. The paper is acid-free and lignin-free.

CONTENTS

1. INTRODUCTION

The Lost Symbol contains a big surprise. Not only is the lost symbol found within the context of the novel, but according to Dan Brown this lost symbol is out there for every one of us to find for ourselves. This is a book which he wants to have real impact on our lives. For some readers it may even be life-changing—and that's not what we expect of a thriller.

Readers haven't known quite what to make of *The Lost Symbol*. Early reports—for example reader reviews on Amazon—have shown in roughly equal numbers reviews which are very positive and those which reveal the reader's disappointment or confusion. There seems to be a consensus of sorts that as a thriller this book is better than the average page-turner, but that it nonetheless has plot holes and shortcomings. For many it does not live up to expectations, though in view of the plot weaknesses of all previous Dan Brown books it is perhaps surprising that the expectations were so high.

Yet there is something about *The Lost Symbol* which lifts it from the status of just another fast-paced thriller to something which warrants consideration as a serious work of literature. For in this book the characters go in search of what is in effect a Holy Grail—the lost symbol—and in a break with the tradition of the genre they really do find the lost symbol. By the end of this book this symbol is not only found but is made available to every reader. It is a quest both for the characters and for the readers, and a quest where for both the goal is really reached. If you read *The Lost Symbol* you too can find the Lost Symbol—and perhaps it can change your life.

My view is that *The Lost Symbol* is no ordinary thriller, and those who seek to evaluate it solely as a thriller miss the point. Rather this is a book where we are invited to follow the hero Robert Langdon on a journey of personal development, a voyage into the mysteries of faith.

In *Finding Dan Brown's Lost Symbol* I offer some additional information and reflection aimed at following up on the quest set by Dan Brown, and perhaps helping a few more people find what Dan Brown is showing us. Taking *The Lost Symbol* section by section this book offers an exploration of Dan Brown's themes, his plot and characters, and explores some of the references in this work which Dan Brown calls "fact-based fiction". It looks also at his presentation of the Masons and how Dan Brown's own life influences his book. Most of all it looks towards finding the lost symbol, helping to unlock the potential of the novel and bring to the fore its message of hope for humanity.

Plot Overview

The plot of *The Lost Symbol* is complex, not always convincing and not what the book should be judged on. Indeed the plot is not in itself particularly important, but rather acts as a functional vehicle for the quest to decode the clues which lead to the Lost Symbol, a reason for a chase across Washington, and sets the stage for the mystic climax. It will make a great action film, but it does not stand up to close scrutiny. The plot may be summarized as follows:

> Robert Langdon receives a call from a man he believes to be the assistant of his friend Peter Solomon, Smithsonian director and senior Mason, asking him to stand in for a speaker who is sick at a lecture that evening. A subsequent call from the supposed assistant asks him to bring with him a box Solomon entrusted to him some years ago. Langdon travels by private jet to Washington and arrives at the lecture location—in the Capitol—as the lecture should be starting. He finds there is no lecture, but instead the severed hand of his friend, and a telephone call from the kidnapper—Mal'akh—demanding that in order to ransom Solomon he should find the burial place of the "Ancient Mysteries". The CIA director Inoue Sato arrives within minutes. Using the clues of tattoos on Solomon's hand Langdon is able to lead her to a sub-basement of the Capitol where they find the Masonic Pyramid. Sato becomes convinced that Langdon is keeping secrets from her and arrests him; Bellamy—a friend of Solomon and fellow Mason—makes his entrance and, believing that Sato is in league with Mal'akh, disarms Sato and runs off with Langdon and the pyramid.
>
> Langdon and Bellamy flee to the Library of Congress. Langdon realizes that the kidnapper threatens also Solomon's sister Katherine, and is able to phone her and warn her. In an elaborate sub-plot we see her work which is in a revolutionary new area (Noetic Science), the murder of her laboratory assistant, her escape, the destruction of her laboratory, and her flight to the Library of Congress to make contact with Langdon. Langdon begins to decode the Masonic Pyramid.

Katherine Solomon meets Langdon in the library. Chased by the CIA, Bellamy uses himself as a decoy and is caught, though not before he has got a message to his friend Colin Galloway asking him to help the fugitives; Langdon and Katherine escape by taking a library book transport conveyor belt to a neighboring building. Langdon makes further progress in decoding the pyramid. Langdon is contacted by Galloway, and with Katherine takes a taxi to meet him. However Katherine realizes that the taxi driver has revealed their location to the CIA. They abandon the taxi at Freedom Plaza, set up a false trail which the CIA follow, then proceed to meet Galloway at Washington Cathedral.

With Galloway's help further progress is made in deciphering the Masonic Pyramid. Bellamy realizes that Sato is not in fact working with Mal'akh and therefore directs Sato to Washington Cathedral. Langdon and Sato again flee, and in the Cathedral College kitchen make more progress at deciphering the Masonic Pyramid, finding what they think is an address (8, Franklin Square). Sato catches up with Langdon and Katherine. She sets up an operation to capture Mal'akh at 8, Franklin Square. Peter Solomon is now known to be at Mal'akh's home (and Mal'akh believed to be absent) and Langdon and Katherine are sent there with the intention of persuading Peter not to speak about what has happened until Mal'akh is caught.

Arriving at Mal'akh's home both Langdon and Katherine are caught by Mal'akh, who has returned and murdered the CIA agents there. He tortures Langdon in order to discover what he believes is the final secret of the pyramid (which Langdon reveals needs an order eight Franklin magic square to decode it), allows the injured Peter Solomon to meet his sister, then with Langdon imprisoned (in a sensory deprivation tank filled with a breathable liquid) and Katherine bleeding to death leaves with Peter for the Masonic Temple. Sato finds Langdon and Katherine, and from Langdon learns where Mal'akh and Peter have gone. In the Masonic Temple Mal'akh reveals himself to Peter as Peter's son Zachary, and wants Peter to kill him on the Temple's altar in a parody of Abraham's intended sacrifice of Isaac. As well as destroying Peter's family he intends to destroy Masonry and create a national security crisis by revealing through transmission of an internet file the prominent Americans who are Masons. For Mal'akh this is an act of evil intended to make him honoured among the demons. Instead of murdering Mal'akh, Peter turns away his hand, breaking the knife rather than kill his son, but a clumsy operation by the CIA leads nonetheless to Mal'akh's death. Mal'akh's soul goes to hell.

The final chapters explain that Mal'akh had failed to publish his information about the Masons, and the national security crisis was therefore averted. A secret backup of Katherine's data means that the loss of her laboratory is not fatal to her research. Langdon, Peter and Katherine are in surprisingly good health. Peter manages the final decoding of the Masonic Pyramid explaining that it is a literal map leading to the location of a Bible buried in the cornerstone of the Washington Monument, as well as a mystic device telling of the Ancient Mysteries contained in the Bible and other scriptures but lost to most in our age. Dan Brown's authorial voice suggests the time is almost upon us when the lost symbol will be found by humanity.

The Reviews

*The Lost Symbo*l takes a proficient reader 10 to 12 hours to read, and critical reflection must take at least a further few hours. Yet many of the first critical views which have determined the critical reception of the book were in print within a very few hours of publication. They were at least half written before the reviewer had even seen a copy of the book. The people acclaimed by our media as the great critics of our age, at the pinnacle of the discipline of literary criticism, have been forced by the unrealistic demands of instant reviewing to write what they must themselves come to realize are ill-considered comments attacking a piece of literature which, while it has many weaknesses, is also in parts brilliant.

First into print just hours after publication of *The Lost Symbol* was the *New York Times*, which produced the well worn phrase that the book is "impossible to put down". Maybe—though I've come across readers who have found they have got lost with the metaphysical themes and actually found it all too easy to put down. The same reviewer also grumbled about the lack of logic in the motivation of the characters. Again maybe this is right, or maybe an attentive reading would have explained the motives. Almost as quick into print was the *Los Angeles Times*. According to their reviewer the book is a "page-turner", but their grumble was that there are "clunky moments when people sound like encyclopedias". They didn't need to read the book to make these generic Dan Brown comments. Other reviewers have given vent to the rather nasty spirit of wanting to throw cold water on a literary achievement. Top marks for spite go to the critic in *The Daily Telegraph* who said the novel was "not quite the literary train-wreck expected". Did anyone other than this critic expect a train-wreck? The *Financial Times* reviewer clearly fails to engage with the novel and comments that it “asks nothing of the reader, and gives the reader nothing back"—the reality of course is that this novel both asks much and gives much. He goes on to make it clear that he has totally missed the message of the book by stating it "is filled with cliché, bombast, undigested research and pseudo-intellectual codswallop". *The Guardian* critic suggests that Dan Brown should write no more novels. *The Observer* continued the fashion for ill-considered bad reviews: “the writing is generally bad in an uninspired way”, which seems to raise the intriguing possibility that this critic thinks it is sometimes possible for writing to be both bad and inspired. The *National Post* critic at least came up with an observation worthy of consideration—that Mal’akh bears a similarity with Thomas Harris’s villain in his 1981 novel *Red Dragon*. A shining exception to the often bitter reviews is provided by *Time* "It would be irresponsible not to point out that the general feel, if not all the specifics, of Brown's cultural history is entirely correct”. Here we at least have a reviewer who accepts that Dan Brown gets a lot of things right a lot of the time.

Of course there are parts of *The Lost Symbol* I don’t like. I’m irritated by his frequent breaches of the rules of English punctuation, where the use together of “?!” is never possible. The book is not helped by some of the factual errors that have got through the editorial process. The island of Siros is in the Aegean Sea, not the Adriatic as Dan Brown asserts.

Turkey indeed has a toe-hold in Europe, but no-one treats the European bit of Turkey—Rumelia—as part of Eastern Europe, as Dan Brown does. It would be possible to argue that the book needed a last revision to remove a few passages that don't seem relevant, and perhaps even to change the title, for surely the book is about the Lost Word, not the Lost Symbol. But no critic can read 500+ pages without finding something they don't like. It is indeed easy to find fault, and that is what most of the over-prompt newspaper reviews have done, preferring a cheap journalistic put down to a proper analysis of the qualities of the book. In their hurry to meet deadlines most critics seem to have missed the point of the book; it is hard to escape the view that many of them had not even read it.

For *The Lost Symbol* is a good book, a book with a message. It speaks to our age—as to an extent do the previous Dan Brown books, though this one more so—and it is this relevance that will ensure it is a best seller as were the previous books. For us today *The Lost Symbol* is worth reading and worth proper consideration. Whether the book is more than just a good read for now is a judgment for later ages. It has within it themes which speak to the human condition, and the possibility must be that future generations will view it as a seminal book of the early twenty-first century sparking discussion that goes well beyond the realms of a simple thriller. Just possibly in *The Lost Symbol* we have a landmark book.

Fact-Based Fiction

In his genre of "fact-based fiction" Dan Brown has tapped something within the human psyche that we should have known all along—most of the time people don't really want to read fiction. And for that matter most of the time people don't want to read fact. One genre is too light-weight; the other too solid. Dan Brown offers us fact-based fiction.

Fiction went through a golden age in the nineteenth and twentieth centuries, but perhaps a change in direction is now called for, requiring a swing back to the roots of fiction: for the very earliest fiction was indeed fact-based. The novel as a genre developed from such sources as exchanges of letters between two protagonists, and from personal journals. In the early novels we believe we are reading something which really happened, and in some cases this is really the case and the story is substantially a true story. What is described in the letters or the journals are real events which happened in much the way they are set out. However as the genre of the novel developed the trend was towards asserting that a story which is made up is in fact true, often with an introductory letter or preface stating how the author has come by the manuscript or the information. Of course we know such books are fiction, but it is possible to suspend disbelief and allow ourselves the luxury of believing that an author's imagination is the real world.

Much of the twentieth century has seen a conscious stressing of the fictional nature of the writing. Everyone who reads Agatha Christie's *Murder on the Orient Express* should be aware that it is just fiction, with characters who never existed and an imaginative re-interpretation of the setting, the Orient Express itself. Agatha Christie was writing primarily for entertainment, and producing novels (of greatly varying quality) at an amazing speed. Ultimately the genre of fiction in which she was writing has given rise to the escapist novel, including such light hearted offerings as those published by Mills and Boon. Today the bulk of fiction purchased is featherweight escapism. Clearly there is a place for this—for if nothing else it sells—but many have a yearning for something more. We want our fiction with some facts in it! We want Dan Brown!

Non-fiction is undergoing a parallel move from academe towards the mainstream. Of course there is plenty of serious scholarly material published in academic journals and monograph series read by what John Milton would call a "fit audience, though few". The tiny sales of many of these ivory-tower academic publications testify to their specialist nature. Rarely do scholarly books make it onto the best-seller list, or indeed even into the non-specialist bookshops. What we are seeing is the development of a huge genre of popular non-fiction. Inevitably the style is journalistic, and inevitably the academic world protests at simplification and an overly broad scope. The reality of course is that such books are being read and discussed, while the vast majority of purely academic work languishes largely unread. There will always be the place for the specialist item presenting the findings of primary research with appropriate academic detachment, yet it is popular non-fiction that is the growth area. Today most non-fiction is more broad-brush, more thought provoking, simply a better read than the traditional academic work. Authors adopt a style of writing which presents a non-fiction theme in a manner accessible to the general reader.

What we are beginning to see is books which blur the boundaries between fiction and non-fiction. Good fiction exploits concepts from non-fiction. Good non-fiction is as readable as fiction. Dan Brown rides the wave of the new genre. His fact-based fiction is of course fiction, but sufficiently factual that we can all learn a lot from it. And his ideas are thought provoking, challenging, and because of their presentation within the format of a novel which everyone is reading they really do lead to popular discussion. *The Lost Symbol*, because of its genre of fact-based fiction, has the potential to do far more teaching than almost any non-fiction book published in the same year.

Characterization

We experience a book through its characters. Yet for a 500+ page book there are remarkably few of them. The only one we have met before in the Dan Brown novels is the hero, Robert Langdon, described as a Harvard "symbologist". His academic discipline of "symbology" is of course itself a fiction, though aspects of the discipline described are parts of history and theology. The majority of the action of the book takes place through Langdon's eyes.

The three members of the Solomon family are key to the story. Peter Solomon is Langdon's friend of many years, secretary of the Smithsonian, and Grand Master of a Masonic lodge. His sister Katherine Solomon, like Peter living in Washington, is described as a Noetic Scientist. In contrast with Symbology, the discipline of Noetic Science does indeed exist. Zachary Solomon, son of Peter, appears under a number of aliases. He is variously Mal'akh, Anthony Jelbart, Andros Dareios, Inmate 37, and Dr. Christopher Abaddon. Linked with Katherine Solomon are her assistant Trish Dunne and the hacker Mark Zoubianis who does a favor for Trish.

Four CIA officers are named. The intimidating and abrasive Inoue Sato is Director of the Office of Security. Named staff who work for her are Nola Kaye, a CIA analyst, Rick Parrish, a CIA security specialist, and Turner Simkins, CIA field operations leader. Staff at the Capitol are led by Warren Bellamy (who like Peter Solomon is a Mason); also named are Trent Anderson, Capitol police chief and Alfonso Nuñez, Capitol security guard.

Of other characters named the most important is Reverend Dr Colin Galloway, who is dean of the Washington Cathedral, and a Mason . He plays a key role, but is introduced late in the book and then largely disappears from the action. We also see in what are in effect walk-on parts:38 Jonas Faukman, *New York Times* editor and Omar Amirana, cab driver.

Of these, only seven or eight in any way hold our interest: Robert Langdon, the three Solomons, Trish Dunne, Inoue Sato, Warren Bellamy and perhaps Colin Galloway. None of these are rounded characters, and we don't learn what makes any of them tick. Indeed they can seem little more than caricatures. None shows character development. Mal'akh's spiritual development is set out, though even here it is unclear how much is new and how much existed even in the young Zachary Solomon and is simply being revealed. It is easy to argue, as several critics have, that the characters are "dud", but this probably misses the point. The book is not a Shakespeare play or a Jane Austen novel and does not intend to provide fully rounded and evolving characters. Indeed this would be a distraction.

Dan Brown's selection of names is significant. Mal'akh is explicit in giving the reason for his assumed name—a form of Moloch, one of the devils in John Milton's *Paradise Lost*. The surname Solomon may suggest a rich American family with Jewish roots, but it also suggests King Solomon within whose capital city of Jerusalem Milton tells us Moloch built a temple. Peter Solomon is therefore a type of King Solomon. Peter and Katherine are traditional names within the Anglo-Saxon name-stock, while Zachary is a rather old fashioned Old Testament name traditionally favored by Puritan families. By contrast the laboratory assistant Trish has a modern name which suggests a less august lineage than the Solomon family. In Zoubianis, Dan Brown seems to have given full reign to his imagination, as this surname does not appear established. However the world has quite a few men called Trent Anderson, Alfonso Nuñez, Omar Amirana and Jonas Faukman—let's hope they all enjoy their new-found fame!

The CIA

Reviewers (and particularly the pre-publication commentators) have been quick to spot that the book is about Masons. Indeed this was public knowledge long before the book was published. They have been much slower to spot that the book is also about the CIA. And while the Masons are presented in a very positive manner, the presentation of the CIA is far from positive.

In CIA director Inoue Sato, Dan Brown has created a most unattractive and unlovable character. She is short, ugly, scarred, poorly dressed, and with a voice that sounds like a man's. In another character these qualities could be a springboard for our compassion, or invoke our sympathy for someone who has undergone brutal treatment for a terminal cancer, or be aspects of a warm and decent person. However none of these apply to Sato. She is abrasive, offensive, rude, intimidating—indeed her only redeeming features seem to be around her competence at her job and her ability to get results, though even these come into doubt during the action of the book. She over-rides rules, uses people as pawns and is willing to see the assassination of Langdon in order to retrieve the Masonic Pyramid, though she is careful to avoid authorizing this action in such direct language. Additionally she smokes—in Dan Brown's world a crime equated with "eco-terrorism"—and she swears.

Sato creates many of the problems within the book. Her abysmal people skills and her willingness to threaten and intimidate discourage co-operation, yet it is co-operation that she needs to resolve the problem. She is so offensive that she is not trusted. First Bellamy and then Langdon come to the view that she is working with Mal'akh, with the result that Bellamy assaults her and Langdon flees from her. Langdon's initial distrust of her leads to his decision to withhold the information that he is carrying Peter Solomon's talisman (the gold cap to the Masonic Pyramid) while later he sees her actions as attempted theft of the Pyramid. Had Bellamy and Langdon trusted her enough to work with her it is possible that the crisis would have been resolved more quickly, that Mal'akh would have been caught (which would certainly have been a better result for him) and possible that some or all of the murders he commits could have been avoided. She is the wrong person in the wrong job.

Sato's ability to access tapped telephone calls may well be a realistic power of the CIA, but it is frightening in that it makes her seem all-knowing. Peter Solomon has been judged a threat to national security (and I'm not sure that why this is the case is ever explained in the book) and as such her office is able to access calls from his phone. She arrives in the Capitol minutes after the severed hand is deposited there, and throughout the evening her use of phone intercepts is her primary information source. Ultimately she uses her CIA power to disrupt internet transmission by closing down part of a network, and while we may be pleased that she succeeds in stopping this particular transmission, her power so to do is perhaps a cause for concern.

The handling of Warren Bellamy by the CIA is harsh. He has run from them and arrest is certainly reasonable, but manhandling him to the extent that he is caused pain and the curious technique of blindfolding him do not seem acceptable—indeed the treatment seems to breach his human rights. His interrogation is not at the CIA headquarters at Langley, just outside Washington DC, but in an unofficial locked building to which the CIA have demanded access. There are no witnesses, no recording, just Bellamy and Sato. Bellamy believes that he is about to be tortured by Sato. In the event he is not. She does however intimidate him, for example by holding a lighted match close to his face while he is blindfolded. Bellamy, an educated Washington professional, believes it likely that a senior CIA officer will carry out unauthorized torture. The plot element only works because American readers will consider it not wholly unbelievable that the CIA may engage in torture. Dan Brown is certainly tapping into an American willingness to believe the most terrible things of the CIA.

The **Central Intelligence Agency (CIA)** is the civilian organization responsible for collecting and analyzing information relating to American national security, particularly information about foreign governments, foreign businesses and foreign individuals. It was created in 1947 as a replacement for an earlier wartime Office of Strategic Services, though its role and remit has been modified many times since. On the CIA's website www.cia.gov it states "The CIA is an independent agency responsible for providing national security intelligence to senior US policymakers. The Director of the Central Intelligence Agency (D/CIA) is nominated by the president with the advice and consent of the Senate. The Director manages the operations, personnel, and budget of the Central Intelligence Agency."

Many of the CIA's activities are covert, including paramilitary operations. Additionally it exerts foreign political influence through a Special Activities Division. Recently the CIA has faced a barrage of accusations in the US and worldwide that its tactics include:

- extraordinary rendition of people to countries where they will be tortured
- torture by the CIA, particularly water-boarding
- assassination
- human experimentation

A survey of these issues may be found on many websites, including *Wikipedia*. Irrespective of the validity of these claims many in America and worldwide believe them to be true. There are claims that the CIA conducts operations without telling Congress, and that there have been a series of operations in recent years which have been kept completely secret from Congress.

The CIA's headquarters is at Langley, Virginia, just outside Washington DC. It employs an estimated 20,000 staff (though the figure is classified). Its most recent known annual budget is for 1998 when it was $26.7 billion. Guesstimates for 2009 are in the region of $100 billion.

2. From the Preface to Chapter 16: The Invitation

The early chapters lead up to the finding of the "hand of the mysteries": the gruesome invitation that leads Robert Langdon, the CIA and the Masons on Mal'akh's quest for the Ancient Mysteries. These opening chapters are also Dan Brown's invitation to his readers to read on through his 500+ page door-stopper.

After brief acknowledgements (a section that few readers of the novel will ever read, nor indeed do they need to read) and a dedication (to his wife, Blanche) Dan Brown presents a bold quotation from Manly Palmer Hall's *The Secret Teachings of All Ages*:

> To live in the world without becoming aware of the meaning of the world is like wandering about in a great library without touching the books.

Few will know this book, but the quotation (in fact from Hall's description of his own book rather than from the book itself) is undeniably exciting. The implicit promise is that in *The Lost Symbol* we will do more than just wander about the great library—that we will indeed find the symbol. This is the promise and it is fulfilled.

Organisations that Dan Brown Says Exist

We have a work of fiction that starts with information which implies it is non-fiction. Dan Brown is keen at the very outset of *The Lost Symbol* to set out his case to be taken seriously. The literary device of listing at the start of his novel that the organizations he writes about are real is one he has used previously—indeed it is almost a Dan Brown trademark. It still needs to be taken with a pinch of salt. The organizations are:

- The Freemasons. No surprise here—of course they exist. Strictly Dan Brown writes not about Freemasons but about Scottish Rite Masons—a group which also exists. Many Freemasons would be keen to draw the distinction.
- The Invisible College. Dan Brown slips this one in. Unless he knows something I don't the Invisible College does not now exist. It existed (briefly) in Britain in the first half of the seventeenth century and was a precursor to the Royal Society. But it is long, long gone. Dan Brown clearly states that it exists, present tense. I think he's wrong.
- The Office of Security. This exists.
- The SMSC. The Smithsonian Museum Storage Centre certainly exists, but the abbreviation SMSC seems never to be used. Indeed SMSC usually means Short Message Service Centre, which is where text messages go between leaving your phone and arriving wherever they are going.
- Institute of Noetic Science. This exists.

The Thriller's Start

Chapter one grabs our attention with an initiation ritual within a Masonic lodge. Few people—other than Masons—are aware of what goes on inside Masonic lodges. The secrecy surrounding Masonic ritual has meant that such rituals have been slow to come to public attention, though today the text of the rituals is published and there has even been some filming within lodges. Parthenon Entertainment's television series *Freemasons Legends Revealed* has been broadcast in both the UK and the USA and contains real footage of Masonic ritual, as does the same company's *Freemasons on Trial*. The Masonic mask of secrecy has slipped, yet still a simple textual description of a Masonic ritual has the power to surprise.

While *The Lost Symbol* as a whole shows Masonic organizations in a favorable light, the initial scenes are ambivalent in their presentation. The ritual is scary—it is of course supposed to be! The idea of life as a preparation for dying leads to the use of symbols of death, including in this ritual a human skull. Later in the book Robert Langdon puts forward ideas which probably reflect those of Dan Brown. Christians pray before the image of a man dying in agony on an instrument of torture, and have as a central ritual the eating of bread and drinking of wine which is variously believed either to symbolize or to physically turn into human flesh and human blood. By contrast with these actions Masonic ritual can seem almost benign. Yet most readers will I think be at least unsettled by Dan Brown's (broadly accurate) presentation of a Masonic ritual. It is perhaps what is termed later in the novel one of the "bad bits" in Masonry. The oaths which are an integral part of the Masonic rituals seem particularly distasteful. They certainly breach the Biblical guidance against taking oaths encapsulated in *James* V:12. Additionally, while it is not directly stated, many feel that the implied meaning is that if you break your word you will be murdered in the nasty ways set out by the various oaths. In some legal codes this may be regarded as an incitement to murder—and perhaps goes a way to explain much of the secrecy around Masonry.

The start of the book also presents Mal'akh, a character who is presented without redeeming features. In *The Da Vinci Code* Dan Brown's bad guy is an albino, a plot device which sparked protests from organizations supporting people who suffer from albinism. In Mal'akh much of the sinister atmosphere is created by his whole body tattoos. Dan Brown is quick to tell us that tattooing is prohibited in *Leviticus* XIX:28, which it certainly is, though the book of Leviticus has some strange prohibitions. Mal'akh's legs are tattooed to represent the twin pillars which feature in all Masonic Lodges—and which themselves represent the pillars of Solomon's temple. They are therefore a symbol at the same time Jewish, Christian and Masonic, and with positive associations. However Mal'akh's tattoo iconography has perched on top of the pillars—on his chest—a great double headed phoenix. This symbol has a precise meaning. In

Masonic terms a double headed eagle is effectively a symbol of Freemasonry, and many nations including the USA have used this culturally positive symbol as a part of their national heraldry. The phoenix often has positive associations, for as a bird which can die and live again it is a symbol of Christ and of resurrection. However the double headed phoenix is regarded as a parody of both the double headed eagle and of the phoenix and is an occult symbol linked with Satan. Mal'akh is taking the Masonic pillars and topping them with a symbol of the devil. His tattoos which present the devil dominating Masonry mirror his infiltration of the Masons.

It would be easy to regard the presentation of Mal'akh in the opening pages of the novel purely as an evocation of a psychopathic villain, a well-worn type in novel and film. Yet there is more than this. From the outset we have a thread of theology which runs through the novel. Mal'akh believes in God and believes in the devil. Indeed he is surely the most devout character in the novel, for his belief is far stronger than that of anyone else. His decision, fuelled by his hate, is to serve the devil, and in the opening chapters of the book this is exactly what we see happening. He has lied (repeatedly) to the Masons; he has a narcissistic appreciation of his own body, and most shockingly he claims to be an angel. His view is expressed in blasphemous terms "angels and demons were identical", and he uses for himself a name which mirrors this ambiguity. Mal'akh certainly brings to mind John Milton's devil Moloch (the derivation that

Mal'akh gives for his assumed name) but to those who read their Old Testament the last book called *Malachi* also comes to mind, and while this book was once attributed to a prophet called Malachi, it is now usually attributed to a nameless prophet inspired by a messenger angel, in Hebrew *mal'akh*. Potentially Mal'akh is named after either a devil or an angel and it may be that the sadness of his story is that he doesn't take the angel as his model. The very start of the book presents issues of theology and this is appropriate, for while the genre is that of a thriller the book is ultimately about theology.

The opening chapters give two sorts of plot elements:

- Our hero Robert Langdon has been summoned to Washington and the Capitol by a simple deception. From the opening chapters we infer—correctly—that Mal'akh needs him, and as the book progresses Langdon does indeed play the role that Mal'akh had wanted.
- Mal'akh has reached the very highest level of Masonry, and may be expected to know the secrets of the group. Yet the early chapters tell us that Mal'akh has been told no secret. As the plot develops we find that the secret is known to all and isn't something that can in any simple sense be told—rather it is lost because it is told of through parables and myths.

Langdon and mystical theology are the two elements that hold this book together. Langdon the symbologist interprets the symbols of mystical theology, though Langdon himself struggles with the nature of the lost symbol.

The book starts not with a corpse—as do *Angels and Demons* and *The Da Vinci Code*—but with a severed human hand. It is tempting to infer that the man must also be dead, though this is shown to be wrong. The brutality of the opening consists in the introduction of the gruesome severed hand with its esoteric tattoos, a hand quickly identified (by the ring it is wearing) as coming from Langdon's friend Peter Solomon. The book leaves much to our imagination. The process of tattooing the hand is not described, nor is the action of severing it, and the reader is spared close consideration of these horrors. Perhaps in this omission we have a hint that *The Lost Symbol* is not intended as a horror story—though there are horrors within the story.

All Dan Brown novels have a heroine who is educated, self-reliant and a scientist. In this book the heroine introduced in these opening chapters is Dr Katherine Solomon, sister of Peter Solomon. Readers of previous Dan Brown novels know that she will be brave and resourceful, that she will join Langdon on the chase, that her life will be threatened, and that she will be saved at the eleventh hour. Katherine Solomon plays true to type. All that is missing is a romantic entanglement with Langdon. Perhaps we are supposed to have read *The Da Vinci Code*, the action of which is a short time before this book, and know that Langdon is romantically committed elsewhere. Or perhaps within the six hours of the plot of this book (for most of which time Langdon and Katherine are apart) even Dan Brown absolutely couldn't shoe-horn in a romance. Maybe the film makers will do better!

Robert Langdon

Dan Brown faces the familiar problem of all writers of book series—how do you introduce to readers who have not read your other books characters and stories from previous books without boring the people who have read those earlier books?

Robert Langdon, the hero of *The Lost Symbol* is also the hero of *Angels and Demons* and *The Da Vinci Code* and so is known to more than a hundred million readers and even more film goers. He is better known than many real-world presidents and prime ministers. Yet Dan Brown does feel the need to introduce him. He is a professor, with many of the eccentricities of the job. His trademark is his Harris Tweed jacket (made of wool produced and woven on the Scottish islands of Lewis and Harris), undoubtedly a useful uniform for a professor in that it combines respectability with the durability needed for the classroom.

Langdon is not a well rounded character—and he's not meant to be. We do start the book with a flashback to an unpleasant experience of Langdon's in Paris, and in earlier books we learn that as a child he fell down a well. Langdon suffers from a degree of claustrophobia, disliking lifts, underground places and anywhere confined, precisely the sort of place Dan Brown likes to put him. But his claustrophobia is mild, and never stops him acting. Perhaps the idea is to suggest that the clever and resourceful Langdon has weaknesses. He is not an Indiana Jones.

The idea that in Langdon, Dan Brown has written about himself is persuasive. Dan Brown has enormous sympathy with Langdon, and seems never to criticize him. Langdon's role as a Harvard professor is a type of lifestyle that Dan Brown would have seen at Amherst, and which in a more junior role Dan Brown himself filled as a teacher at Exeter.

A particular function of Langdon, loved by readers but hated by critics, is that he is used as the mouthpiece for encyclopedic passages. Readers seem to love this casually acquired knowledge, much of it trivia, though newspaper reviewers of this and all Dan Brown novels seem uniform in their view that it s a flaw. I guess it is the difference between giving readers what they want, and giving people what the critics say the readers want, and Dan Brown opts for the former. We see Langdon as encyclopedia when he encounters the hand of the mysteries. For starters he can identify the gruesome object. When he first sees the tattooed crown and star we are told "these symbols had appeared together many times in history, and always in the same place—on the fingertips of a hand. It was one of the ancient world's most coveted and secretive icons. The Hand of the Mysteries" (chapter 13.) Now did you know this? I'm guessing almost no readers did, but encyclopedia Langdon is on hand to fill us in. Occasionally Dan Brown's authorial voice plays encyclopedia, as "The Capitol's massive footprint measures more than 750 feet in length and 350 feet deep. Housing more than sixteen acres of floor space, it contains an astonishing 541 rooms." (chapter 4) Again I didn't know this detail—I just think of the Capitol as big.

Quite where Langdon ends and Dan Brown begins is a challenge for all readers. Perhaps the success of the books with Langdon as their hero comes from this autobiographical element.

Items of Interest

Manly Palmer Hall (1901-1990) quoted at the start of the book was a twentieth century Prospero who sought to combine the wisdom of philosophy, religion and science. He was a prolific writer, with over 200 books to his name, who believed that wisdom could be found in the myths, mystery and symbols of the ancient Western mystery teachings, and this wisdom then embodied in people's lives. He termed this *Ancient Wisdom*, and while his writings on the topic are extensive it seems possible to sum up his thinking in just one of his lines:

Hence the disciple of the Ancient Wisdom is taught to realize that man is not essentially a personality, but a spirit.

His *magnum opus* is *The Secret Teaching of All Ages*, an encyclopedic survey of Western Mysticism and a truly enormous book privately published at his (considerable) expense in an 8-point typeface. Many of Dan Brown's ideas in *The Lost Symbol* seem to originate in this volume, and it is therefore fitting that he acknowledges this debt in his prefatory quotation. The concept of knowledge being lost though in full view—a key theme of *The Lost Symbol* - is one noted by M P Hall, who writes:

> I felt strongly moved to explore the problems of humanity, its origin and destiny, and I spent a number of quiet hours in the New York Public Library tracing the confused course of civilization. With a very few exceptions modern authorities downgraded all systems of idealistic philosophy and the deeper aspects of comparative religion. Translations of classical authors could differ greatly, but in most cases the noblest thoughts were eliminated or denigrated. Those more sincere authors whose knowledge of ancient languages was profound were never included as required reading, and scholarship was based largely upon the acceptance of a sterile materialism.
>
> (*The Secret Teaching of All Ages*)

M P Hall writes also of what he terms in a book title *The Secret Destiny of America*, suggesting that America was selected by the ancients for a philosophical empire. His extensive work in Masonic history and philosophy appears to have led to his recognition (1973) as a 33º Mason in the Scottish Rite. The Philosophical Research Society of Los Angeles which he founded (1934) promotes the "ensoulment" of all arts, sciences and crafts.

The **Falcon 2000EX** in which Langdon flies to Washington is a very nice executive jet with a short to medium range. It certainly functions as a means of getting Langdon to Washington, flying at speeds of just under Mach 1. But this plot element stretches our credulity. No academic is flown anywhere in an executive jet like this. Academics in UK and US mostly fly economy class, while a big-name Harvard professor—someone like Langdon—might just merit an upgrade to club class. Presumably the explanation is that Dan Brown likes fast planes, for it is hard to see how the Falcon 2000EX is a necessary or even credible plot element.

The **Institute of Noetic Sciences** was founded 1973 to carry out research on human potential. Among its founders is Apollo XIV astronaut Edgar Mitchell who has spoken of his personal experience of God on the return journey from the moon to the earth:

> The presence of divinity became almost palpable, and I knew that life in the universe was not just an accident based on random processes ... The knowledge came to me directly.

The institute is located in California, just north of San Francisco. It wasn't particularly well known, but Dan Brown's The Lost Symbol will surely change that. Its purpose is set out on its website:

> The institute's work is dedicated to transforming contemporary worldviews on the relationship between consciousness and matter. The implications of our empirical research and community education efforts extend far beyond the laboratory and the lecture hall. Indeed, our work speaks to a shift involving humanity's

deepest knowing and understanding of ourselves and our universe.

The story of the **Angels of Mons** provides an example against which to examine Mal'akh's statement that **one man's angel may be another man's demon**.

The Battle of Mons, August 1914, was the first battle fought between Britain and Germany in the First World War. It was a British victory won against the odds. Britain's force of 70,000 was outnumbered more than two to one by Germany's 160,000, and left exposed by the retreat of the Belgian and French armies. Britain's 300 guns were faced by 600 of Germany, while the German army included cavalry divisions which Britain did not have. A Germany victory should have been inevitable, yet Britain won. British losses were shocking enough at 1,638 dead, but the German losses, though seemingly not accurately recorded, were roughly treble.

There is no obvious reason for Britain's victory in this battle. Both armies were professional and both avoided mistakes. Germany had a great advantage in manpower and equipment and should have had an easy victory. The explanation then given was supernatural. The story is that British troops returning from the battle reported that a host of angels fought alongside them and given them the victory. Some of the stories specifically say that the angels were led by St George of England, and some that the angels fought with bows and arrows. Of course the British newspapers loved the story. It suggested that the war was a just war, with God and St George helping Britain fight an evil enemy, that British soldiers were in the words of the hymn "Christian soldiers, marching as to war, with the cross of Jesus going on before". The story did much to encourage British volunteers to enlist, to do their bit to "fight the good fight". The story of the angels of Mons endured throughout the war as an inspirational story for the British troops.

Today we surely regard the story of the angels of Mons as rumor and propaganda. Yet at the time it was confidently believed that a host of angels had fought alongside the British. If this really was true then the German soldiers were attacked by a supernatural force which they could hardly have regarded as angels. What the British perceived as angels the Germans must have perceived as demons. If the story of the Angels of Mons were true (and surely it is not) then one man's angel would have been another man's demon.

3. CHAPTERS 16-38: BENEATH THE CAPITOL

The symbolism of the location of these chapters should not be lost. Dan Brown takes the action into the foundations of the central building of the US government, the Capitol. In *Angels and Demons* he took the action into the foundations of the Vatican, to the very grave of St Peter on which St Peter's Basilica is built, and similarly in *The Lost Symbol* he is in effect playing around with the history of the foundation of a powerful entity, here the United States of America. It is appropriate that the Masonic Pyramid should be concealed beneath the heart of the US government. It is appropriate too that the drama - which is potentially the biggest national security crisis in America ever - takes place in this central location.

Dan Brown locks his fiction into fact by presenting readers with the ground plan of the basement of the Capitol building. (between chapters 32 and 33) The device blurs the boundary between fact and fiction though it seemingly serves no other purpose. The precise location of room SBB XIII is not a plot element, nor is finding a path through the Capitol a theme of the book. Possibly the ground plan stresses the size of the Capitol (for those who missed Dan Brown's encyclopedic description of a building with 16 acres of floor space)—but we don't need it to read the book.

We are specifically told that the layout of the sub-basement is identical to a fourteen tomb mausoleum. This sounds as if it should be significant, but I can't find the point. Rather I feel I'm in a fog of Dan Brown's fact-based-fiction. I don't think the plan is "identical"—fourteen tomb mausoleums had fourteen tombs, while the sub-basement has thirteen rooms. Leaving this aside I wonder if there is really a suggestion that the sub-basement of the Capitol was modeled on a mausoleum—and presumably intended to house bodies. It seems unlikely—unless Dan Brown has some supporting evidence. Here (and at some other points in the book) I wonder if Dan Brown toyed with plot elements that in the event he didn't use. Some sort of mausoleum built for the founding fathers of America—and then not used—would be a fascinating concept, and in many ways fits with the train of thought that sees the American state founded by Masons as part of a grand scheme of history.

Complying with the Demands of a Terrorist

Langdon asks a key question about whether SBB XIII should be opened on Mal'akh's demands:

> "Wait! ... Think about it. Peter gave up his right hand rather than reveal whatever might be behind this door. Are you sure you want to do this? Unlocking this door is essentially complying with the demands of a terrorist." (chapter 35)

Sato's brusque response quashes the question. Yet it is a key one. Mal'akh wants the pyramid, but is unable to get it out himself. In opening the door the CIA do indeed comply with the demands of a terrorist. Had the door remained closed the pyramid would have remained outside Mal'akh's reach. It is difficult to play the game of "what if?" but it does seem that Mal'akh would have delayed bringing matters to a head—or at least communicated further to try to persuade the CIA to open the door. With the information they had from phone taps, catching him was in this scenario possible. We find later that Mal'akh desperately wants the information from the Masonic Pyramid in order to make himself (in his view) perfect—he would have waited.

Notwithstanding Langdon's doubts, Sato makes the decision which is in effect to comply with the demands of a terrorist. Her stated motivation is to stop Mal'akh carrying out his threat and to catch him, both laudable aims, yet the case for co-operation with him as the means to further these aims is not convincingly made. Nor is it clear that it is a right policy. Indeed it may be that Langdon really was correct. His sense of right and wrong seems superior to the moral rationalizing of the CIA.

The Powers of the CIA

The plot element that is key to understanding the book (but which is given minimal space in the story) is that the CIA have intercepted the calls that Mal'akh (impersonating Peter Solomon's assistant) has made to Robert Langdon. Sato brushes off Langdon's question about who informed her that he was coming to the Capitol with the abrupt "Where I got my information from is not your concern". (chapter 19)

The implied scenario is alarming—the CIA is monitoring Peter Solomon, and by implication is monitoring anyone of his level of importance. How many Americans is the CIA monitoring? How many people around the world are being monitored? Should we be concerned?

Now *The Lost Symbol* is just a work of fiction, yet it presents its audience with the scenario of the CIA routinely monitoring the telephone calls of very many Americans. Dan Brown clearly feels that his readers will find this credible. In this case the CIA on the basis of what is presumably just a routine monitoring trawl has pulled up a reference to the Capitol building, and a reference to a lecture at a particular time. This information has been stored. When an event happens within the Capitol building at this precise time the event and the telephone log are put together almost instantly, and the CIA representative—Inoue Sato—arrives on the crime scene within minutes of it happening. This is impressive surveillance. It is a marvelous tool in the fight against crime, but it also has worrying implications for civil liberties.

The book you are now reading contains references to the CIA. It is distributed in both paper and electronic formats. Does the mention within it of CIA mean that it will be trawled? Does this matter? If you are reading it on Kindle, does the CIA know you are reading it? If you bought it online has the CIA tracked the purchase? Is big brother watching us all?

Washington

Dan Brown touches briefly on the well worn story of the Masonic affiliations of many of the founders of America. This is not new material. That many of the signatories of the Declaration of Independence were Masons is well-established and in no way surprising. This was an age when most professional men were a member of the Masons—what would have been strange indeed is if few or none of the signatories had this membership. Some have expressed surprise that the major buildings of Washington had their foundation stones laid in Masonic ceremonies. Again this should not really be a cause for surprise. Masons would take an interest in the construction of major state buildings. Yet fortunately Dan Brown avoids the excesses of the conspiracy theorists.

He also avoids basing his plot on curiosities of the Great Seal of America as shown on the $1 bill, though he references these through a distraction created by Katherine Solomon. Quite why the Great Seal should feature an unfinished pyramid of thirteen steps topped by an all-seeing eye is a puzzle which Dan Brown clearly feels he will not solve. That a six-pointed star based on the pyramid points to letters which spell "Masons" is dismissed by Langdon as simply coincidence, which it probably is.

Trish Dunne

The murder of Katherine Solomon's assistant Trish Dunne is carried out with remarkably few pages devoted to it and remarkably little emotional involvement from the readers.

Trish has been presented as a likeable character and a resourceful worker. Yet as with most of Dan Brown's characters we really know very little about her. The most memorable event is her death, drowned by Mal'akh in a massive ethanol tank used to house a specimen of a giant squid. We are given just a few words in the authorial voice setting out her fear as she drowns and the pain of her death and are left with the grotesque image of her body in the ethanol tank on top of the giant squid. Her death seems more of a plot device than a reason for our grief.

Trish is simply the woman in the wrong place at the wrong time. Mal'akh had expected to find only Katherine at the laboratory, and he sees Trish as a "liability"—a calculating word to describe a human life. His decision to murder her is unpremeditated and improvised, and as such all the more chilling. If the reader had any doubts about his intentions in visiting Katherine this surely dispels them—Mal'akh is there to murder her.

The Chamber of Reflection

This room—SBB XIII - is something of a loose end in the plot of *The Lost Symbol*. We don't get an explanation as to why this room exists, or why Peter Solomon maintains such a room in the basement of the Capitol. There is no convincing reason for how someone could rent a room which virtually becomes lost within a building. Possibly we are to infer that the sub-basement has been closed off because it is damp, yet the paper-trail of recording occupancy and paying rent should surely alert the Capitol's estate management staff to the circumstance of someone using the room. Presumably Peter Solomon must have set up a system for passing information about the room to a fellow Mason in the event of his death, so that the Masonic Pyramid would not be lost, though it is particularly hard to see how occupancy of a Capitol room could be kept secret in these circumstances. Perhaps we are not supposed to speculate.

As a plot element somewhere is needed to conceal the Masonic Pyramid, somewhere which Mal'akh cannot enter, and this is how the room functions. Why the Pyramid is behind a curtain within the Chamber of Reflection rather than in full sight is not explained. Langdon in his role of walking encyclopedia tells us what the room is, but this is a long way from truly explaining the room. Undoubtedly this is a Masonic "Room of Reflection" where men may meditate on life and death, and where various symbols, all explained by Langdon, serve the role of *memento mori*—but are we really to speculate that Peter Solomon on occasions slipped down to a hidden sub-basement in the Capitol in order to reflect on mortality? His Masonic House of the Temple was close by, and its Room of Reflection far more easily entered.

Item of Interest

Dan Brown doesn't know how to text! He sets up a text message exchange between Mal'akh (impersonating Peter Solomon) and Katherine Solomon. While we are told that Peter is a novice at texting, Katherine is supposed to be proficient in this modern art. Yet she texts (chapter 25):

> peter, congrats on learning to text! relieved you're okay. spoke to dr. A., and he is coming to lab. to see you shortly! -k

A reasonably proficient texter would produce something like this:

> peter congrats on learning 2 txt relieved u r ok spoke to dr a & he is coming 2 lab 2 c u shortly k

The first is 123 characters; the second 99.

4. CHAPTERS 39-55: THE LIBRARY OF CONGRESS

As Robert Langdon flees from Sato and the CIA, the action of the book moves from the constricted spaces of the basement of the Capitol to the uplifting expanse of the reading room of the Library of Congress, sometimes considered the world's most beautiful room. The ideas presented likewise move to grander themes as Langdon begins to decode the Masonic Pyramid. The book has started with M P Hall's quotation comparing our experience of life to being in a great library, and here Dan Brown truly places us in one of the world's greatest libraries.

What would you do?

Dan Brown sets up a situation where Robert Langdon must act instantly. Warren Bellamy bursts into room SSB XIII, overpowers Anderson and Sato, and orders Langdon to "Grab the pyramid! ... Follow me!" (chapter 41) Would you follow him?

Langdon has two sets of concerns about Sato's handling of the affair:

1. He believes that Sato is giving in to the demands of a terrorist, and that this is wrong. He also believes that Sato is violating Peter Solomon's privacy, and again that this is wrong. He is not

convinced that what they are doing will help find Peter.

2. In the minutes immediately preceding Bellamy's arrival Sato has crossed several lines in her dealing with Langdon. She has accused him of lying and of obstructing an investigation (both false accusations), she has arrested him, and she has done this by aiming a gun at him, an action which is totally unnecessary as Langdon is effectively imprisoned in the Capitol—indeed it serves only to intimidate, and suggests that Sato is acting outside the rules.

Langdon appears to consider the possibility that Sato may be complicit in Peter's kidnapping. Probably most readers think this also. He does have good reason to be concerned about Sato's behavior.

Set against this is the seniority of Sato's office and the authority she undoubtedly holds. Running from a CIA director is a very serious offence. Indeed it may be a plot hole of the novel that Langdon is not subsequently in trouble for this. Most Americans seem to have a thorough awareness of the authority of the police and of organizations such as the CIA, and do know that to ignore the police or run from the CIA is simply not acceptable or safe. The American instinct is to obey the CIA, whether out of respect or fear.

Dan Brown tells us Langdon justifies his action with the phrase "His gut told him to trust this stranger" (chapter 42). In many ways his gut seems right. Almost immediately the stranger introduces himself, in marked contrast with Sato's failure to give a proper introduction. Bellamy acts the good guy he is; Sato though perhaps on the side of the angels does not act in a way to inspire trust. Human beings will rightly trust the likes of Bellamy.

Katherine Solomon's Escape

It is Robert Langdon who is responsible for warning Katherine, and it is solely because of his warning that she escapes. The plot is strained at this point. It is amazing that while fleeing the CIA he has the time and the presence of mind to ring an editor to get her number, then ring her. He even suggests where they can meet, though it isn't clear that he knows where Bellamy is taking him.

The result is that Katherine is able to escape from Mal'akh. The scene takes place in the pitch black, which is great within the context of a novel but will provide a few headaches for the film makers. Katherine shows determination and bravery; Mal'akh shows cunning and an ability to improvise. Katherine indeed escapes, though Mal'akh destroys her laboratory and (apparently) all her data.

Decoding the Pyramid

Within the context of the chase that is now underway it is strange indeed to see Langdon and Bellamy sitting down in a room they both know the CIA will soon access, decoding the Mason's Cipher on the pyramid.

The Mason's Cipher is of course very simple to decode. This very simplicity hints at the existence of multiple levels of complexity in the Masonic Pyramid, exactly the sort of ideas found in legends about it. While Langdon succeeds in cracking the Mason's Cipher, what he finds is just a group of seemingly random letters. The first layer of the code is easy—but seemingly yields nothing.

More Theology

Bellamy asserts that the Ancient Mysteries exist, and that there is an ancient knowledge that can imbue mankind with great power; Langdon is a skeptic. Bellamy's response is through Bible quotes. This is a key episode in the book, delivered against the drama of the breathless chase and the horror of Mal'akh's violence, and it rewards close reading. What Bellamy is saying is dramatic, and it is backed not by obscure quotations from little read parts of the Old Testament but rather by quotes from the mainstream. The two key ones are:

> God created man in his own image (Genesis I:27).
>
> The kingdom of God is within you (Luke XVII:21).

The idea is that the human soul is a divine spark, a light within. Here and elsewhere Dan Brown supports the idea with Bible quotations. (It should be noted that *Luke* XVII:21 is more often translated "The kingdom of God is among you"; however "in, within, inside" is the primary dictionary definition of the preposition *entos*, and "among" not a usual meaning.)

In a parallel plot thread we learn of Katherine Solomon's work in Noetic Science, and the sort of questions she is both asking and answering. These are:

> Does anyone hear our prayers? Is there life after death? Do humans have souls? (chapter 52)

The questions Bellamy and the Masons are thinking about dovetail with these questions that Noetic Science is asking. What the Masons see as "the secret is how to die" (Prologue) is truly a vital secret because there is a life after death. The Masons reflect Christian belief in "God created man in his own image" and "the kingdom of God is within you", while Noetic Science shows that humans have souls. The true implications are realized by Mal'akh: "they will start to find their way". (chapter 52) For Mal'akh the discipline of Noetic Science is as dangerous as the religious truths held by the Masons in that both systems answer all three of Katherine's questions with a yes. If we are sure that prayers are heard, that there is a life after death, that we have a soul, then we live our lives differently. Indeed we begin to find our way to God.

As so often in *The Lost Symbol* it is Mal'akh who gives the key theological insight. We are on the brink of an age when because of contributions of both science and mysticism we are about to see a new world order. The lost symbol is about to be found.

Zachary Solomon

The development of Peter Solomon's only son, Zachary, is shown in a series of flashbacks. It reveals a central problem with the human condition in that evil seems to come from no-where.

Zachary is born into a wealthy family. We are led to assume that he has an excellent education; we know that he grew up in a beautiful home. His parents are happily married, and he is loved. While some of the book implicitly criticizes Peter's parenting it is hard to see just where he goes wrong. Peter may not be in all ways perfect, but he doesn't commit a grave error either. When Peter comes of age he gives him a large sum of money. We see how this affects Zachary and may therefore tend to criticize the action, but an impartial assessment sees nothing wrong with the action. Zachary is the beneficiary of a loving family and an excellent material start in life.

He is clearly a rude young man and can appear as the spoilt rich kid. When he receives his inheritance he spends it thoughtlessly. These are faults, but they are not in themselves evil actions. So far Zachary is simply a wayward youngster. Even his drug involvement is ambivalent. Of course drug taking is legally wrong, but within the context of massive drug taking in the Western world it seems a step too far to call it evil. His arrest by Turkey (presumably as he was leaving Turkey for Bulgaria, though Dan Brown doesn't actually make this clear) is in fact most unlikely to be for his own personal use of drugs, as Turkey has little interest in arresting a departing Western tourist with a small quantity of drugs. Rather it would seem to be an arrest for drug smuggling. This frontier is a stage on the drugs route—typically Afghanistan, Iran, Turkey and Bulgaria, and once within the European Union to any part of the EU. Presumably Turkey has arrested a drug trafficker. However the plot is weak here as Zachary is very wealthy and does not need the money a drug trafficker can earn—his action seems motiveless.

While the details are unclear the result is not—Zachary ends up in a rather unpleasant Turkish prison. His father flies in to help, and Zachary learns by an overheard conversation that his father will get him out through legal means (in about a week) rather than through the dangerous and illegal method of a bribe, which would probably secure his release the next day. For Zachary this is the turning point in his life, and from this time onwards he acts in ways which are evil. Yet where this evil has come from is inexplicable.

The conversation between Peter Solomon and the prison warder is narrated as Mal'akh recalls it. Peter has flown to Turkey to support his son and to secure his release. His request to speak with his son is refused by the warder. Rather the warder is aware of the Solomon wealth and wants a bribe to get his immediate release—and this bribe is refused. The stated reason, as overheard by Mal'akh, is that Peter will not teach his son that money solves all problems.

There is an implied sub-plot which is not actually made explicit within *The Lost Symbol*. We are told that Peter is in Turkey seeking the release of his son and that with the Solomon influence and using American consular channels he can bring this about in around a week. This would be a good result through legal, official channels with a reasonably sure expectation of the release of his son. The process would also mean that the treatment of the American prisoner would matter to the Turkish authorities, so that significant abuse of Zach Solomon during the remaining week in prison was unlikely. By contrast paying a bribe to the prison warder would put Peter outside the law, and pose additional problems to them both in leaving the country. While it may be that a bribe culture exists in Turkey as the book sets out, giving a bribe is far from safe. None of this is set out in the book, yet it is hard to escape the view that the sensible decision for Peter is exactly the one that he takes. When the prison warder asks for a bribe Peter cannot say "I don't trust you"—that would be the way to get his son abused - but instead gives the view that Zachary Solomon must learn that he has done wrong. It is a right answer.

The upshot of the conversation that Zachary has heard is that he knows his father is in Turkey and is working to get him out of prison, and that this will take perhaps a week.

There is no evidence from the text that Zachary was experiencing particular abuse. While he clearly had an unpleasant week ahead of him it was in the end only a week. But instead of waiting patiently Zachary devises a scheme to buy himself out. This involves the brutal murder of another prisoner. While the book skirts around the edge of this atrocity it seems that it is Zachary and the prison warder who together murder the man, and damage his body to the extent that it is unrecognizable and may be passed off as that of Zachary. Shortly afterwards Zachary commits a second murder—of the gaoler. This double murder is his transition from out of control youth and criminal drug-trafficker to the evil of premeditated murders.

Items of Interest

The word **pyramid** brings to mind the Egyptian pyramids, though many cultures both old world and new world have used them. Egypt has well over a hundred pyramids, Sudan nearly as many, while locations as varied as Mexico, India and China all have pyramids. Technically these are right-square pyramids, with a square base and four triangles which join at a point. Because the weight is distributed over a large base they are exceptionally stable, and can therefore be built on a massive scale. This feature was presumably discovered independently in many cultures leading to the building of pyramids wherever human civilization reached a certain level.

The Great Pyramid of Khufu in Cairo is the only one of the seven wonders of the ancient world still standing, and even today among the largest of man-made structures. It was for long the world's tallest building. The pyramids have prompted plenty of questions about how they were built, as well as questions about why so much effort was expended in creating these buildings. Persuasive is the idea that the Egyptians regarded the pyramids as "resurrection machines" enabling the soul of pharaoh to ascend to the realm of the gods.

The **Masons' Pyramid** is known only to legend, yet the idea that the Masons might select the structure that is a pyramid for an important object is persuasive. The Pyramid symbols stability, human reasoning and human faith reaching up towards heaven, all qualities respected by Masons. Every one dollar bill in America includes a picture of an unfinished pyramid. The idea seems to be that the early American state saw itself as in the process of constructing a perfect, finished pyramid, a perfect society.

Mason's Cipher is used for the message engraved on the stone pyramid. It is (as Langdon rightly notes) very easy to decipher. It is a simple substitution cipher where each symbol relates directly to a letter of the alphabet—or in other words Mason's cipher is itself an alphabet. Indeed it is so simple that it frequently appears in books about codes written for children. Freemasons have certainly used it, particularly in the eighteenth century, and it may have served to give a degree of security to a short message. As an alphabet comprising straight lines it is easy to inscribe, which may be an additional appeal to Masons.

An alternative name for the cipher is "Pig Pen cipher". The idea that this is because some of the letters look like pig pens seems fanciful—rather a proper etymology might indicate where this cipher came from, and perhaps also why the Masons liked it so much.

5. CHAPTERS 56-79: ON THE RUN

This middle section of *The Lost Symbol* utilizes the familiar device of the chase. It is a two stage chase. Langdon and Katherine are running after Mal'akh in order to ransom Peter. The CIA are running after Langdon and Katherine in order to get to Mal'akh, though for the CIA Peter's life is incidental.

The chase theme is familiar from countless films, from cartoons, from thrillers without number. Dan Brown is using a well-worn technique and it works.

Is there no help for the widow's son?

This is the centuries-old cry of a Mason needing help from fellow Masons. Masonic ritual suggests and some writing about Freemasons sets out that it was first used by King Solomon following the death of his friend Hiram Abiff, though why Hiram Abiff should be called a widow's son is far from clear. More plausibly it refers to the story of Elijah raising from the dead the Widow's Son, as told in *1 Kings* XVII 17-24. Here help is given where no help can reasonably be expected. The Mason uttering this cry for help is appealing for similar exceptional help where all other help is past.

In *The Lost Symbol* the cry for help is made by Bellamy, and answered by Galloway. It is carried by an intermediary, Bellamy's assistant, who does not at first understand the message, though thanks to the wonders of Google he soon finds out what it signifies. The message (in the book and doubtless in the real world) satisfies the basic requirement that it should express extreme need, and that it should not be immediately understood by any intermediary.

Galloway is not the cavalry. Rather he is an old man, completely blind, and with no particular skills to help two people on the run from the CIA. What he does offer is sanctuary within the church of which he is dean, and by talking with them helps them find some answers. Curiously Langdon and Katherine could have found sanctuary in many other places and been safer. They might have checked in to an hotel. They might have travelled up and down a metro line. As the weather seems warm they might even have sat on a park bench. In the event all these places would have been safer than Washington Cathedral, because Bellamy guesses where Galloway would meet them and Bellamy can tell Sato. While Langdon and Katherine think they will find sanctuary at the Cathedral this is in the event not in fact what they find. They do however receive some answers, as Galloway realizes that his role has moved from gatekeeper of the Ancient Mysteries to guide to reach the Ancient Mysteries.

"Men do the unthinkable when pushed to the brink"

In this sentence (chapter 57) Mal'akh gives his father an explanation for his actions. Seemingly this is how he justifies to himself his decision to conspire with the prison warder to murder a prisoner, and his subsequent murder of the warder. Mal'akh is suggesting that when in a Turkish gaol he was pushed to the brink. It seems unlikely. We have seen that Zachary started life with loving parents, a good education, and a substantial bequest when he came of age. This is a superb start in life. We have seen that he has become a drug addict, and presumably a drug pusher as well (else as an American it is unlikely that the Turkish authorities would have put him in prison). In prison he overhears his father speaking with the prison administrator, learning that his father has come to Turkey and is working to get him out. His father's decision to go through the legal system rather than to pay a bribe (with all the risks this involves) is what Zachary sees as unforgivable. It is this action which he claims pushed him to the brink, and fuelled years of hatred.

It is not clear that Zachary truly was pushed to the brink. In any case this was years before his attack on the Solomon family and murder of his grandmother; he is certainly not pushed to the brink at that time. He is however on a physical and metaphysical brink—the brink of the ravine, and the brink of a new stage in his life. Presumably Dan Brown has deliberately set up this event to take place in a way to recollect the time when Zachary was a child, for the location is Zach's Bridge. While the bridge has perished the name remains on a bolder: "Zach's bRiDge". Quite what we are to make of the juxtaposition of correct use of the apostrophe with an inability to use upper and lower case letters correctly I'm not sure, but perhaps the idea is that it is representative of the innocence of childhood.

There seems to be absolutely no reason why Zachary turns out as he does. The idea of a societal cause—of being pushed to the brink—is not credible. Rather in Zachary we seem to have an individual who actively chooses evil.

It's all Greek to me!

Dan Brown's knowledge of Greece and Greek seems dodgy. He describes the Aegean Sea as "ink-blue" (chapter 57) when the conventional description following Homer is "ink-dark". Syros, where Zachary settles is in the Aegean Sea (not as stated in the Adriatic), and while the cuisine of the Greek islands has much to commend it, the description as "sumptuous" seems wrong—rather it is a homely, peasant food. The one dish named—arni souvlakia—is usually spelt arni souvlaki. The community on Syros named as Possidonia is almost always transliterated as Poseidonia, the place of the god Poseidon. Calling it a "town" is misleading—it has a population of around 3,000. Zachary becomes Andros Dareios, which we are told means "wealthy warrior" (chapter 57). But it doesn't! Andros is the genitive singular of the noun man. Dareios is a Greek form of the Persian Dara, king, used by Herodotus as the name for the Persian leader defeated by Alexander the Great, Darius. If it means anything (and really it doesn't) the translation is something as nonsensical as "the Darius of a man". Dan Brown mentions Mykonos as a place visited by Zachary without referencing its best known and un-missable feature—that this tiny community is one of Europe's leading gay resorts. Dan Brown also seems to be at sea with the Greek alphabet. The final decoding of the symbols on the base of the pyramid requires that the Greek letter H should be read as an H in our alphabet—when in fact it is an E. The Greek alphabet does not have a letter to represent our H, but it does have an aspiration mark ᶜ which could have been used.

Problems of this nature don't help *The Lost Symbol*. Nor does his frequent use of the idiosyncratic (and wrong) punctuation "!?"—English punctuation permits only one to be used. This reflects the syntactic consideration that a clause in English may be interrogative or exclamative, but cannot be both. Dan Brown's punctuation is sloppy and plain wrong, and in view of the enormous sales of his books will lead more people into the temptation to misuse the tools of English punctuation.

Items of Interest

Dan Brown's foray into the work of **Albrecht Dürer** may be regarded either as a characteristic encyclopedic excess of the author—or just possibly an important contribution to understanding the theology of the book. Dürer (1471-1528) is usually considered to be the greatest north European artist of the renaissance. A polymath of his age, Dürer combines a vast inter-disciplinary knowledge with artistic genius to produce works which continue to challenge. The work featured in *The Lost Symbol* is *Melencolia I*, which is a large and complex engraving. It is frequently reproduced, though usually at a smaller size than the original, with the result that the engraving seems dark and cluttered. It is hardly attractive to the non-specialist; the specialists have written many books on it, and assure us of its worth. The picture shows a winged figure in a state of despondency, probably to be identified as human genius unable to soar upwards unaided. Around the figure are a collection of objects which need to be understood as allegorical. They cannot be interpreted in any simple way, and it is far from clear that they fit within any one single allegorical framework. It may be that the picture should be interpreted as Dürer's spiritual self-portrait. He feels melancholy because his spirit, however aided by the insights of the renaissance, cannot fly up to God. Within the conceptual framework of Dan Brown's novel this is a picture of the soul trapped because the symbol has been lost.

Magic Squares are familiar curiosities. One of the best known is the Indian lucky square called Kubera Kolam:

27	20	25
22	24	26
23	28	21

In this magic square all the directions including the diagonals add up to 72. It is associated with prosperity.

Dan Brown reproduces parts of a **black magic ritual** in his description of the transformation of Zachary into Mal'akh. (chapter 77) The ritual he uses comes from *The Key of Solomon the King* translated by S. Liddell MacGregor Mathers (1888). This book is a grimoire—a sort of magical grammar which sets out how symbols may be put together. The book is claimed to be by King Solomon, and most of the magic within it is claimed to be white. However the translator reproduces two books of black magic—which he calls "evil magic", stating that these are not in fact by King Solomon though attributed to him, and advising "I cannot caution the practical student too strongly against them ... Let him who, in spite of the warnings of this volume determines to work evil, be assured that that evil will recoil on himself and that he will be struck by the reflex current".

(Preface) It is material from one of these black magic books that is reproduced in Mal'akh's ritual.

It seems likely that Dan Brown has a copy of *The Key of Solomon the King*. The title brings to mind the title under which *The Lost Symbol* was originally going to be released: "The Solomon Key". Perhaps at one time he considered using the so-called "white" magic of this book as the codes on the pyramid. What he has in fact done is used much of the black magic detail to shape the laboratory and practices of Mal'akh. This adds verisimilitude to the book, and it is hard to see how else he could have achieved the spine chilling world of Mal'akh, but it is also distasteful as a dabbling in the occult.

William Shakespeare found verisimilitude in a similar place in *Macbeth*. Here the incantations of the three witches are taken from a genuine Satanic mass, and his decision to perform part of such a ritual on stage has shocked all those who realize what it is. It is also effective in that the witches scenes in *Macbeth* are truly spine chilling. Because of this *Macbeth* has an enduring reputation as an unlucky play, and many actors will not even call it by name, speaking instead of *The Scottish Play*.

6. CHAPTERS 80-95: "THE MASONIC PYRAMID HAS ALWAYS KEPT HER SECRET ... SINCERELY"

This section of the book is characterized by uncertainties. Bellamy comes to feel that he has been wrong and that Sato is right, though most readers will feel in their hearts that Bellamy was right and Sato wrong. Langdon peels through more layers of code on the Masonic Pyramid without reaching the true secret. Galloway realizes this and seems pleased. Though he has previously described himself as a guide rather than a gate-keeper he seems to have retained some of the gate-keeper function, and feels that Langdon and Katherine should go so far in their decipherment, but only so far. His intellectual joke on "sincerely" is one that Dan Brown used in *Digital Fortress* and obviously likes. Sincerely literally means "without wax", and a perfect stone carving un-patched with wax was "sincere", therefore true and perfect. The joke is strained when applied to the Masonic Pyramid as the secret is kept with wax, not without wax.

Power without Accountability

Inoue Sato's interrogation of Warren Bellamy is chilling. The concern comes not from what she actually does as from her implied threats and the strong sense that her power knows few bounds. She does not seem to have a boss to hold her to account.

Bellamy has been handcuffed. As he was apprehended while fleeing, this is understandable. He has also been blindfolded. No reason is given for this and it is particularly strange as he has not been violent towards his captors—the implication is that it was done solely to soften him up for his forthcoming interrogation. He is not deliberately hurt but he is roughly handled to the extent that he gets some minor bruises. The interrogation takes place in an unauthorized place—a government building that Sato enters out of hours using the authority of her credentials—and Sato is the sole interrogator. Sato has a level of seniority where she is in effect representing the establishment and her actions appear to be those that her establishment thinks are appropriate. We therefore have a situation where Dan Brown believes his readers will believe that the USA government at a senior level authorizes unofficial interrogation techniques, and tolerates a class of senior CIA people who seem to be able to act without accountability.

Sato's interrogation of Bellamy is reasonably civilized. However she quickly gets to the stage of saying "I am asking you to trust me on this." (chapter 80) The CIA is in effect saying, "trust us, we're the CIA". Bellamy's response is almost comic: "Well, I don't!" If you do trust the CIA their actions here and throughout the book seem justified. If you don't then they are sinister. The key question seems to be "who guards the guardians?"

The Theology of the Rev Dr Colin Galloway

Galloway's starting point is the question "Is it not possible that we are still living in the Dark Ages?" (chapter 82)

The ages of civilization have long ago been established by Christianity and centuries ago modified by historians. The starting point is the idea of the Middle Ages—the ages between the resurrection of Christ and his second coming. Within a Christian system we are still in the Middle Ages. Historians have tampered with this simple concept. The years up to the fall of Rome (AD 410) are regarded as the Classical Age. The Renaissance starts (depending on what country you are interested in) at varying dates from the late fourteenth to early sixteenth century, and is regarded as the beginning of the Modern Age. That leaves for the Middle Ages a thousand years or just over—in Britain for example the period AD 410—1485. Even this period we've cut down. 1066 or thereabouts onwards is the High Middle Ages, which leaves AD 410 -1066 as the Dark Ages. Yet even here current thinking is that the Dark Ages weren't really as dark as we once thought, and the specialists are less happy with the term. We are very close to saying that the Dark Ages didn't really exist.

In asking if we are still living in the Dark Ages Galloway is asking if we are still living in what Christian thinking regards as the Middle Ages. Implicitly he is suggesting that the achievements of the Renaissance, Reformation,

Enlightenment and modern Science have missed a key truth. He is suggesting we lack an awareness of soul, that each of us contains a soul that returns to God on our death but that many of us do not perceive this. While Bellamy illustrated this with quotations from *Genesis* and *Luke*, it is Langdon who in effect fills in the gaps with additional quotes. One is the aphorism of the Hermetic philosophers: "Know ye not that ye are gods?" Another is an answer to this question: "Ye are gods!" (*Psalms* LXXXII:6) Galloway is talking of a cosmic force which in the words of Albert Einstein "transcends ... dogma and theology".

In the events of *The Lost Symbol* we have an imaginative account of a time when the Middle Ages—Galloway's Dark Ages - comes to an end. Galloway realizes the enormous significance of the time: "I never imagined that I would live to witness this moment". (chapter 84) Mal'akh too realizes the significance of the moment, and his purpose is to prevent it happening, to keep humanity in darkness. What we are seeing in the brief hours of the action of the book is a fight between light and darkness so that the new age may come to humanity, or may be denied to humanity—and at the end of the book with the defeat of Mal'akh something has changed, and that new age is ready to be ushered in.

The Masonic Pyramid

The levels of code on the Masonic Pyramid are indeed complex:

- the 16 letters inscribed in Mason's Cipher: SOEUATUNCSASVUNJ.
- re-ordering of these letters according to the clue of the capstone box and the egraving *Melencolia I* to produce JEOVA SANCTUS UNUS.
- solving the anagram to create ISAACUS NEUTONUUS (treating I/J and U/V as forms of the same letter).
- having the capstone with its visible inscription: The secret hides within The Order.
- heating the capstone to boiling point to reveal an additional line Eight Franklin Square.
- heating the unfinished pyramid to reveal additional symbols under the wax of its base.
- realising that the message of the capstone is that The Order Eight Franklin magic Square is needed to decode the symbols on the base.
- interpreting the symbols when decoded.
- finding a second interpretation for the same set of symbols.
- finding a third interpretation for the very same symbols.

This represents a lot of steps to decode the Pyramid. Curiously the first three are an irrelevant dead end, though I imagine that few readers spot this. The name Isaac Newton is not needed to decode the pyramid, though he does provide a context. Perhaps the idea is that there should be a dead end here, so that someone might think (as Langdon indeed does) that the pyramid is not a real map but a metaphorical map pointing to "One True God".

The remaining steps require that the symbologist should have both the unfinished pyramid and the cap stone, and should be prepared to take the extreme steps of boiling the cap stone and heating the unfinished pyramid. Once the codes have been physically shown to exist their ultimate solution should not be too difficult. A Google search on "Franklin square" will turn up the existence of Franklin magic squares, and armed with this information the decoding of the symbols is reasonably simple. Interpretation of the Symbols—either allegorically as Langdon does, or as a map to the Temple as Mal'akh does, or as a physical map as Peter does—is not so very difficult either. The message of the Masonic Pyramid is kept safe not so much by the complexity of a code—they aren't all that complex if studied with appropriate time—but simply by concealing it with the two parts kept apart.

Sato's Rant

Inoue Sato catches up with Langdon and Katherine close to the National Cathedral. They have laser-sighted rifles aimed at them.

Sato's style is aggressive from the outset: "You've made some exceedingly poor choices tonight." (chapter 91) Her instinctive style is to seek to intimidate. She is also wrong.

Langdon's one true choice of the evening has been to contact Katherine and warn her that Mal'akh is coming to murder her, in doing so saving her life. This aside he has been almost entirely a passenger swept along on other people's agendas. It is Sato who took him to the Chamber of Reflection, Sato who acted as if the villain, Bellamy who rescued him, and Bellamy and then Galloway who led him and Katherine across Washington. Very little within this is choice. Rather he is acting on the conviction that there are good guys—Bellamy and Galloway—and bad guys - Mal'akh and Sato—and within this belief system his actions are pretty much determined. Rather the poor choice was made by Sato who failed in basic people skills so that (despite the respect and instinctive support her senior rank should give) she looked like a villain.

Sato speaking to Langdon calls the problem "the goddamn mess you made" and follows it up with "you've made an ungodly mess". She feels that she had told Langdon in the Capitol building that the problem is about more than Peter and at the level of an analysis of the words she uttered this is true. Yet she is a bad communicator who does not realize that there is a fundamental difference between what the speaker says and what the listener hears. Langdon saw the problem as being solely about his friend and he saw access to the Ancient Mysteries as a way of ransoming him, though also as giving in to the demands of a terrorist. Sato could have said in a few words that Mal'akh as well as threatening Peter was also threatening national security and so shifted the belief system in which Langdon was operating. She didn't, at least not in words that anyone understood.

She then turns on Katherine, and criticizes her for telling the police where her brother was being held a hostage. But how could Katherine have done otherwise? Neither Katherine nor Peter knew how to contact Sato—and anyway they believed she was helping Mal'akh. It is not a useful criticism. Curiously Langdon's arrest seems forgotten. A couple of hours earlier she had arrested Langdon, and he should still be under arrest, and in trouble for resisting arrest. The logical action would be to handcuff him and take him to CIA headquarters. Perhaps Sato realizes that she may still need Langdon and Katherine.

Galloway's treatment by the CIA seems heavy handed. This blind, old man is manhandled by them, despite his protests: "Take your hands off me! ... I'm blind, not inept!" (chapter 92) He is "forced" into a chair and he comments on the large numbers needed to detain an old man.

Sato is still acting as if the villain, and the CIA seems out of control. Galloway makes a decision not to share with Sato and the CIA a further secret of the Masonic Pyramid, stating instead "The Masonic Pyramid has always kept her secret ... *sincerely*". (chapter 92)

7. CHAPTERS 96-122: HOW TO DIE

This section of *The Lost Symbol* is about death. It is also a section about what happens to us after death. The starting point is the conviction that we have an immortal soul. Mystics have known this since the dawn of history. Noetic Science is—according to the book—now able to prove this through the technique of weighing a human soul. Katherine Solomon does this through some precise weighing, though the fundamental context is very simple. A human being is weighed before and after death and the weight recorded at both times. This very simple experiment has been carried out many times in the last couple of centuries with experimenters agreeing that there is a small but measurable loss of weight around the time of death. Experiments on animals do not show such a weight loss. The results seem clear; acceptance of the validity of the results has not generally followed.

Once the soul has left the body it must go somewhere. The theological argument of the novel is that the soul may return to God—that the soul is from God and a part of God. But in the fate of Mal'akh we see an alternative fate, for his soul goes off to hell. Within the theology of the book is the core Christian idea that after death there is judgment, and souls go from the judgment either to heaven or hell. Dan Brown is attempting within his novel to create the sort of vision of death and judgment that is familiar to generations from Michelangelo's Sistine Chapel painting *The Last Judgment.*

Simulated Drowning

Mal'akh's torture of Langdon (and previously of Peter) takes the form of simulated drowning in a sensory deprivation tank. It is an extremely effective piece of writing as most readers will I think believe Langdon is really dead. That such a drowning could be simulated is counter intuitive and the technology that makes it possible is not widely known.

Dan Brown draws the link with water boarding (chapter 112), and produces what is probably the most politically charged reference in the book. Water boarding is a form of torture where a victim is immobilized (usually by being tied to a board) then water poured into the lungs so that the victim starts to drown. It causes fear, extreme pain, frequently lung damage and brain damage, and occasionally associated injuries—the victim in their agony may pull against restraints with sufficient force to break bones. However it usually leaves no visible marks on the body. The CIA was reported in 2007 as using this form of torture, directly authorized by the United States Department of Justice. It was withdrawn in 2009 by President Obama.

In tests victims of this torture capitulate in an average of 14 seconds. It is an effective form of torture, and if there is any possible justification of torture it is that it works in revealing information. Water boarding will work quickly, and usually in a single session. Khalid Sheikh Mohammed is reported as having been water boarded by the CIA not once or twice or even half a dozen times but 183 times. President George W Bush stated that he gave the CIA useful information. Alternatively 183 episodes of water boarding may suggest that this has gone beyond torture as an interrogation device and become torture as a recreation for sadists. Under Obama's government consideration has been given to prosecuting the CIA people responsible, though it seems that this will not in fact happen.

Mal'akh has a refinement of water boarding which Dan Brown suggests may be known to the CIA—certainly he makes it clear that Sato is familiar with it. This is simulated drowning in a breathable liquid—an oxygenated perfluorocarbon. There is a factual basis to Dan Brown's plot line here as breathable liquids really do exist, and are beginning to be used for some medical treatments. Dan Brown links the experience of simulated drowning in oxygenated perfluorocarbon with sensory deprivation—which may be a meditative technique but can also be a form of torture—and adds a graphic description of the trauma felt by an individual when suddenly removed from a sensory deprivation chamber. Langdon's experience is shocking, and the implication of the book that the CIA uses such techniques raises a worrying view of the CIA.

Throughout *The Lost Symbol* it is the CIA who are criticized. Early reviews of the book were keen to discuss it as a book about Masons, yet the reality is that it has at least as much to say about the CIA, and while the treatment of the Masons is largely positive that of the CIA is almost entirely negative. However the criticism is of the CIA as an organization not of individuals within the CIA, not even of Sato. A moment of humor is provided when Langdon within the sensory deprivation tank seeing Sato's face "wondered if he was looking into the face of God." (chapter 112) Sato gets something of a bad press, but this sentence reminds us that within the theology of the book she too carries a divine spark.

Peter and Mal'akh as Abraham and Isaac

The story of Abraham and Isaac is among the strangest stories in the Old Testament—and Dan Brown's use of the theme makes it no less strange.

The story is told in a few brief verses in *Genesis* XXII. Abraham is instructed by God to take his son Isaac onto a mountain and there to sacrifice him. Abraham does as he is told, but at the last moment an angel from God intervenes. Abraham has passed the test. A ram is provided as an alternative sacrifice. There's really very little in the story apart from these bare bones. That Isaac asks why they are not carrying a sacrifice onto the mountain adds drama, while the circumstance of Isaac carrying the wood for the fire has been seen by generations of Bible readers as an event which prefigures Jesus's carrying of the cross on which he will be killed. The story has been a favorite of artists, and pictures abound, usually with the angel catching Abraham's arm as he is about to plunge the knife into his son's chest—a detail which incidentally is not in the Bible.

The story is disturbing on several levels. It speaks of a society where human sacrifice was practiced, where Abraham the patriarch has no fundamental problem with the idea of a human being killed and offered as a burnt offering. And it presents the God of the Old Testament as requiring such a sacrifice. The explanation usually offered for the story is that God was testing Abraham to see if he was worthy, but this isn't what the text actually says. The word used (*Genesis* XXII:1) is "tempted". God tempts Abraham to this act. Abraham's compliance appears prompted by fear, not love.

There is a clear conflict with the New Testament, where we read "God is not tempted of evil, neither tempteth he any man" (*James* I:13). If we are to make any sense of the Abraham and Isaac story we have to see it in terms of a growing awareness of God by the patriarchs of the Old Testament. We hear of "the God of Abraham, the God of Isaac, the God of Jacob" (*Matthew* XXII:32) suggesting that while God is the same, each of these three patriarchs perceives God differently. The story should perhaps be understood not in terms of what God wanted but what

Abraham convinces himself that his God wanted. Abraham thinks that his God requires the sacrifice of Isaac; God sends an angel to stop this unwanted sacrifice. Perhaps the point of the story is the revelation that God does not want human sacrifice.

In the climax of *The Lost Symbol* Dan Brown presents the scenario of a father sacrificing his son. The father, Peter Solomon, is placed in the role of Abraham about to sacrifice his son, here Mal'akh. The parallel with the story of Abraham and Isaac is drawn by suggesting that the very same knife is used. Yet the differences with the Abraham and Isaac story are pronounced. Mal'akh is seeking sacrifice from his pride; by contrast Isaac is presented as meek and compliant (at least in most of the retellings of the *Genesis* story). The *Genesis* story is clear that Abraham intends to go through with the sacrifice by killing his son, yet Peter turns away his hand, breaking the blade of the knife on the stone altar. In view of the evils committed by Mal'akh to the Solomon family this is a remarkable moment of compassion. Peter acts not as an Old Testament patriarch, but as a Christian acting in accordance with the message of the New Testament.

The death of Mal'akh is the most terrifying section in a novel which has no shortage of fear and violence. Mal'akh has intended his death to be part of an act of evil which destroys the Solomon family, exposes Masonry, and causes shock waves which may destabilize America and all those countries in which Masonry is established. It is a culminating act of premeditated evil. There is no societal excuse, no sense of a breakdown or of a mental health problem as an explanation for his actions. Rather his actions are presented as a deliberate journey into evil. He embraces evil, seeing power and blood sacrifice as the rituals which direct his life. His tattoos use his body as a canvas to express the evil he seeks.

Mal'akh's death occurs not in a manner which copies the Abraham and Isaac story, but by natural causes. The broken glass from the skylight of the Temple falls on him causing multiple injuries. Peter correctly assesses his injuries as fatal, and proceeds to speak with his dying son, giving him two key pieces of information:

- You are not perfect.
- You have been loved.

Mal'akh's pride in his supposed perfection is his greatest sin, the sin for which Lucifer and his legion of angels were driven from heaven and became devils. He believes himself to be perfect, with the last symbol—the lost symbol of the title—drawn on the crown of his head. Peter is at pains to say that this is not indeed the lost symbol, and that Mal'akh is therefore not perfect. He is seeking to give his son some humility. That Mal'akh was loved is no doubt true. Within Christian thought it is the love which someone feels and shows for others that leads to their salvation. Being loved may encourage expressing love, but simply being loved is not enough. For Mal'akh's soul to be saved he himself needed to love. Perhaps given time the expression of his father's love could bring Mal'akh to love his father, but Mal'akh does not have time, at least not in this world.

The pain of Mal'akh's death is severe, but short lived. As he dies the pain ceases. And then Dan Brown shows his soul going off to hell, to a place of terror, a hell every bit as terrible as our worst imaginings. In what is surely the most powerful passage in the book (chapter 122) Mal'akh feels "rage" and "confusion", he plunges "into an abyss far darker than any I have ever imagined ... the barren void." He is filled with "boundless fear." Finally "I am facing all the dark souls who have gone before. I am screaming in infinite terror ... as the darkness swallows me whole." The passage is almost too terrible to read. Mal'akh has lived a life of evil without any redeeming feature whatsoever—yet his damnation is a punishment beyond comprehension. Perhaps his hope should be in some harrowing of hell. Perhaps the final words of his father will help him towards humility and to a realization that he is worthy of love.

Items of Interest

Dan Brown gives some brief information about the **Shriners**. The Ancient Arabic Order of the Nobles of the Mystic Shrine is an appendant body of the Freemasons, founded in 1870 as a group stressing fun and fellowship. They have no connection with Arabia or Islam, nor are they

Ancient, Noble or possessed of a Mystic Shrine. They do however have around 375,000 members, and they do wear fezzes. Their charitable activity is centered around the running of twenty-two hospitals for children in the USA, Canada and Mexico, and they have helped hundreds of thousands of children. Dan Brown's inclusion of this group in his book seems accidental. His plot tool of the order-eight Franklin magic square is misunderstood as the address "8, Franklin Sq", and as the Shriners have premises on the square mention of them was perhaps inevitable. Maybe the accidental publicity in *The Lost Symbol* will do this group some good.

Mal'akh claims to have taken his name from **Moloch**, one of the fallen angels in John Milton's *Paradise Lost*. The presentation of Moloch in *Paradise Lost* helps explain what Mal'akh thinks he is doing. In *Paradise Lost* Moloch is the first of the twelve devils who followed Satan, as a travesty of the twelve disciples who followed Jesus. Moloch is described as a king, one who requires from his subject the sacrifice of children, and therefore the tears of their parents. We are told that the noise of the slaughtered children is drowned out by the sound of drums and cymbals. In Milton's words:

> First, Moloch, horrid king, besmeared with blood
> Of human sacrifice, and parents' tears;
> Though, for the noise of drums and timbrels loud,
> Their children's cries unheard that passed through fire
> To his grim idol.

Mal'akh too wants the sacrifice of a child and the tears of parents, though with the twist that it is Mal'akh who is to be the child sacrificed.

Milton tells of the people who worshipped the devil Moloch—the Ammonites—and adds the names of their cities, Rabba, Argob and Bashan (Milton doesn't like -sh- sounds so he calls it Basan), all ultimately defeated by King David. We hear also of Moloch's deception which resulted in Solomon building a temple to Moloch "right against the temple of God" on what the Vulgate calls the "mons offensionis", the hill of offense, Milton's "opprobrious hill". In *The Lost Symbol* it is Peter Solomon who allows Mal'akh to infiltrate the Freemasons building his "temple" within the "Temple", the headquarters of the Scottish Rite Freemasons. The text suggests that Dan Brown really does see Peter Solomon as a type of the Solomon of the Bible.

> Him the Ammonite
> Worshiped in Rabba and her watery plain,
> In Argob and in Basan, to the stream
> Of utmost Arnon. Nor content with such
> Audacious neighbourhood, the wisest heart
> Of Solomon he led by fraud to build
> His temple right against the temple of God
> On that opprobrious hill, and made his grove
> The pleasant valley of Hinnom, Tophet thence
> And black Gehenna called, the type of Hell.

What Mal'akh builds in the pleasant lands of Hinnon and Tophet is "black Gehenna". Milton uses a New Testament word for hell, one which suggests also a place of sacrifice. Mal'akh uses Solomon to build a hell in a pleasant place.

Later in *Paradise Lost* Moloch is described as a "homicide", and this is indeed the crime which appears to have set Mal'akh firmly on the path of evil. In Book 2 we learn of the ambition of Moloch:

> His trust was with th' Eternal to be deemed
>
> Equal in strength, and rather than be less
>
> Cared not to be at all; with that care lost
>
> Went all his fear: of God, or Hell, or worse,
>
> He recked not

Mal'akh likewise wishes to be powerful, a powerful devil, and acts without fear of God, or hell, or worse - whatever worse could be. Yet it is Moloch who presents one of the most vivid descriptions of hell, the hell that seemingly Mal'akh goes to:

> What can be worse
>
> Than to dwell here, driven out from bliss, condemned
>
> In this abhorred deep to utter woe!
>
> Where pain of unextinguishable fire
>
> Must exercise us without hope of end

Mal'akh substance it seems, like that of Milton's Moloch is "indeed divine, And cannot cease to be", and he has the most terrible punishment of everlasting life in hell. Indeed in book six Moloch and other devils are attacked by the angels Gabriel, Uriel and Raphael, and though he suffers the most gruesome and agonizing wounds he cannot die. Rather:

> Down cloven to the waist, with shattered arms
> And uncouth pain fled bellowing.

For those who read and reflect on Mal'akh's passage to hell it is clear that oblivion would be infinitely better.

8. CHAPTERS 123-133: FINDING THE LOST SYMBOL

In the real world as a result of the traumas they have suffered Langdon and Peter & Katherine Solomon would all be in hospital and quite possibly in intensive care. Dan Brown has them running around Washington sightseeing. I suppose we should accept this as a plot device in keeping with the fast pace of the novel and the suspension of belief that is part of the process of reading a novel—but perhaps it would be easier to imagine the events taking place a year later when they have all had some recovery time. However we must believe that Katherine, despite massive blood loss, has only a slight sensation that her legs "still felt rubbery" (chapter 124) while Peter is able to regard his injuries "as if it were nothing of consequence." (chapter 124) Langdon is at least reported as being "utterly sent" (chapter 125) but he still seems to have plenty of energy for a pleasure trip first to the top of the Washington Monument, then as the sun rises to the top of the Capitol.

Loose Ends

The final chapters tie these up reasonably well.

Mal'akh did not transmit his film of powerful people taking part in Masonic ceremonies. The CIA were able to block the transmission.

- Katherine Solomon's data was not lost—her brother Peter had kept a backup without telling her.
- Sato seemingly forgets about the arrest of Langdon. By the rules he should be charged and the charges then either formally dropped or acted upon.
- The sub-plot of the internet posting about something "buried out there somewhere" reaches a conclusion of sorts. This seems to be weak and unconvincing, not Dan Brown's best work.
- The Masonic Pyramid is shown to be important in that it inspires curiosity about the Ancient Mysteries. It is indeed a map, but a map to something we all know about anyway. What is important is the quest, not the destination.

Sato's parting comments give grudging thanks to Langdon for his help, but "with no hint of warmth." (chapter 126) She also manages to give him a brief dressing down. Sato has achieved much in the course of the book, including averting a major security crisis. Her handling has not been perfect and both she and the CIA have seemed intimidating and even frightening, but she has been effective.

The Lost Symbol Revealed

The strongest point of this book is that the Lost Symbol really is revealed:

- At its simplest it is the Bible, buried beneath the Washington Monument.
- It is the scriptures of all religions, all of which have something to say about the Ancient Mysteries, all of which have value, and all of which can be honoured in a Masonic temple.
- It is Jesus Christ.
- It is the message of thinkers and mystics through the ages from Hermes Trismegistus to Albert Einstein.
- It is the human soul, the light within, the God within.

The symbol has been lost in that much of humanity has lost its faith. Scientific empiricism has in many cases replaced belief and mysticism.

Langdon asks the question of why the great teachers of the ages have not proclaimed the truth from the rooftops—why for example in the Bible the truth is hidden in allegory and parable. He reasonably points out that teachers—all teachers—make a big effort to make people understand what they want to teach. The answer he receives from Peter is that the information is dangerous and that it must therefore be kept hidden. This is why teachers have felt themselves unable to broadcast it.

The answer is not really convincing. It seems incredible that through the ages not a single initiate of the Ancient

Mysteries would have broadcast the knowledge they have. Possibly a better answer is the one implied throughout the book—that the message is out there in plain sight, but people chose not to see it.

The Second Coming

The end of our age is forecast. Within the context of the story the assembly of the Masonic Pyramid is indicative of the truth breaking out. The time is right for the Ancient Mysteries to be revealed. Mystic Christianity and Noetic Science concur, and the truth of the Ancient Mysteries can break through. The communications revolution of the internet is fundamental in linking people together and according to Dan Brown fundamental in bringing about the Second Coming. Humanity will come to realize the very areas that Katherine Solomon researched:

- We all have a soul
- There is life after death
- Prayers are heard
- Universal consciousness is real.

The Second Coming is imminent. Dan Brown toys with the date given by ancient South American calendars of the end of our age being 2012—precisely December 21st 2012.

Items of Interest

A key document of **Hermetic** belief is the **Emerald Tablet**. This is a document of the Classical world preserved in Arabic, and subsequently translated into Latin. Isaac Newton is one of the many translators into English of the Latin, and his translation is reproduced below—I've modernized the spelling and tried to use punctuation to help find a sense.

This is an exceptionally difficult document. It is a translation from Greek to Arabic to Latin to English, and it shows its multiple translation layers in its linguistic obscurity. Even with careful reading it is hard to know quite what it means. It does have the idea "as above, so below" and it does say something about the alchemical concept of transmutation.

> It is true without lying, certainly most true: that which is below is like that which is above; that which is above is like that which is below; to do the miracles of one only thing. And as all things have been (arose from one by the mediation of one) so all things have their birth from this one thing by adaptation. The Sun is its father, the moon its mother, the wind has carried it in its belly, the earth its nurse. The father of all perfection in the whole world is here. Its force or power is entire if it be converted into earth. Separate thou the earth from the fire, the subtle from the gross, sweetly with great industry. It ascends from the earth to the heaven; again it descends to the earth and receives the force of things superior and inferior. By this means ye shall have the glory of the whole world; thereby all obscurity shall fly from you. Its force is above all force, for it vanquishes every subtle thing and

> penetrates every solid thing. So was the world created. From this are, and do come, admirable adaptations whereof the means (or process) is here in this. Hence I am called Hermes Trismegistus, having the three parts of the philosophy of the whole world. That which I have said of the operation of the Sun is accomplished and ended.

William Blake (1757-1827) gets a brief mention towards the end of *The Lost Symbol*, with two lines from one of his poems quoted. Curiously these are presented in block capitals, for no reason that I can see. The two lines are frequently quoted in isolation, though they are part of a short poem *The Vision of Christ that thou dost see* which deserves to be quoted in full.

> The Vision of Christ that thou dost see
> Is my Visions Greatest Enemy
> Thine has a great hook nose like thine
> Mine has a snub nose like to mine
> Thine is the Friend of All Mankind
> Mine speaks in parables to the Blind
> Thine loves the same world that mine hates
> Thy Heaven doors are my Hell Gates
> Socrates taught what Melitus
> Loathd as a Nations bitterest Curse
> And Caiphas was in his own Mind
> A benefactor of Mankind
> Both read the Bible day & night
> But thou readst black where I read white

Blake had controversial religious views, though views which chime with those presented in *The Lost Symbol*. He regarded all religion as ultimately the same and that Antiquity (the Ancient Mysteries) therefore preaches the Gospel. On Jesus Christ he writes "He is the only God ... and so am I, and so are you" and "men forgot that All deities reside in the human breast."

9. THE LOST SYMBOL AND THE MASONS

The Lost Symbol has a lot to say about the Masons. It presents striking description of Masonic ritual along with a plot that requires that very senior members of the American establishment are Masons. As in all Dan Brown novels it is hard to know quite where fact stops and fiction begins.

History of the Masons 101

This is an enormous topic, but readers of *The Lost Symbol* do need something on the topic, if only because Dan Brown can at times be misleading. The fundamental problem is that he writes not about Freemasons but rather about another Masonic Group, the Scots Rite, though the difference is not stressed in his writing.

Presentations of the history of the Masons are exceptionally numerous, and range from the driest of fact-based narratives to the wildest of mythical accounts and conspiracy theories. The debates about their history are equaled only by the present debates on their influence within our society. Depending on whom you read you can find that the Masons are either an irrelevant club for old men who like to dress up—pretty much the view of Zachary Solomon—or that the Masons rule the world—which seems to be the view of Inoue Sato, and perhaps also of Dan Brown.

The best known Masonic group is the Freemasons, and sometimes Mason and Freemason are used as if they are synonyms—they are not. A Masonic organization is a group, almost always of men only, who are bound together by an oath and who meet regularly, frequently in a place called a Lodge, and often within a context of ritual. Often there are secret means of recognition and frequently claims of secrets held within the organization. Freemasons are the best known and largest Masonic group and many other Masonic groups grow out of the Freemasons or are modeled on them.

While there are those "historians" who would claim that Freemasonry is as old as Adam, and more than a few who trace its origins to the age of King Solomon or to Ancient Egypt, most (more sober) historians regard Freemasonry as a mediaeval creation. The earliest unambiguous reference to a Masonic organization is in Britain, contained within the *Regius Manuscript* of 1390. There is no reason to think that 1390 is the start date; rather it is well within the realms of possibility that Masonic organizations existed in the British Isles many years before this date. The stories that the Masons came to Anglo-Saxon England in the time of Athelstan or that they are to be linked with the Knights Templar are just about possible, though they are without reliable evidence and therefore not accepted history. Many of the earliest records of Masons are in Scotland. Tradition asserts that the Masons started as a guild of stonemasons, and that subsequently they came to accept people who were not stonemasons within their ranks. The original stonemasons were termed "operative masons"; the non-stonemasons "speculative masons". It is plausible that early Masonic organizations were linked with mediaeval religious dissent and later with the emerging protestant faith. The idea is convincing that the strange garb of an initiate to the Freemasons is in fact that of a mediaeval heretic on the way to the gallows. The concept seems to be that in joining the Masons the initiate had accepted that his actions might end with him on the gallows hung as an heretic.

Freemasons are not specifically protestant—indeed they are not even specifically Christian—but they do have a clear religious requirement that members believe in God. The Roman Catholic Church will not permit its members to join the Freemasons. In Britain and America the majority of Freemasons are protestant Christians.

Because they were secret societies the early Masons have left few records. Properly recorded history starts in 1717 when four London lodges grouped together as the Grand Lodge of England—the Freemasons—and imposed uniformity of practice. These so called Moderns were opposed by Masonic groups who didn't see things in quite the same way, and the Masonic history of the eighteenth century is characterized by a schism between the Modern Freemasons under the jurisdiction of Grand Lodge of England and the Antients—who liked both the archaic spelling of "ancient" and a more traditional form of ritual. In

1813 they were united, and from this time there has been one main channel of Freemasonry.

Characteristic of the Freemasons are the following:

- they have three grades (degrees) of members: Apprentice, Fellow (or Journeyman) and Master Mason.
- they meet in a Lodge.
- they have an extensive legendary history back to 4000BC, which they call Anno Lucis. Dates are calculated from this baseline, so 2009 is to the Masons 6009.
- fraternal relations between members are paramount.
- they have extensive and complex rituals and claim to have secrets.
- they have means of recognition, including the well known Masonic handshake.
- they have a belief in God, and their ritual is heavily influenced by the Christian tradition.

Their purpose is frequently stated as being "to make good men better". Their ritualistic allegory, reflection on death and therefore the importance of living life well, along with their interest in charitable activities, may well mean that their purpose is often fulfilled. For many the Freemasons have been primarily a social club, and in far flung corners of the British Empire the Freemasons were often in effect the sole social club for the British community in a particular location. Over the centuries there have been many who have joined the Freemasons in the hope of self advancement, and it is sure that on occasions the fraternal obligations which many Freemasons feel towards one another have been abused for the advancement of members. Freemasons tend not to regard their organization as secret—after all the buildings that are their Lodges are usually well known, and many individuals make no secret of their membership—yet they are societies with secrets. Robert Langdon uses the example of Coca Cola to explore this concept: Coca Cola have known premises, and people who work for them are unlikely to keep their employment secret, but they do nonetheless have secrets. The recipe of Coca Cola is a secret.

The Freemasons have been enormously successful in attracting members. Today there are perhaps five million Freemasons worldwide, including around two million in the United States and approaching half a million in the British Isles. Their membership was probably higher a century ago, at a time when the global population was much smaller. They tend to attract professional men, so a significant percentage of people in our society who have power are members. The conclusion seems inescapable that the influence Freemasons exert over their members must have a real impact on our world.

There are several organizations which are comparable to the Freemasons. For example, first documented in the eighteenth century (though claiming a much longer pedigree) is the Ancient Order of Druids. Constituted on lines similar to the Freemasons, the Druids were a major social force in Britain in the nineteenth and early twentieth century. They operated as a Masonic organization, as a society providing support to widows and orphans of members, and as a cultural organization that did much to foster an appreciation of the Celtic heritage of the British Isles. Unlike the Freemasons, the Druids declined sharply in the inter-war years, and while they exist today (both in Britain and America) they are but a small organization.

The fraternity system at American universities is frequently Masonic in structure. This is a system where at university many men join fraternities and women sororities which provide variously accommodation, a social club, friendship, pastoral support and just possibly life-long advancement. Dan Brown was certainly a member of the fraternity system at his university, Amherst College, and so has direct experience of an organization Masonic in structure.

A level of complexity within Freemasonry is the lack of an overall governing body. Grand Lodge of England governs Freemasons in England and Wales. Scotland and Ireland have their own Grand Lodges. In the United States each state has its own Grand Lodge. Around the world Grand Lodges tend to be on national lines. In some parts of the world they are called Grand Orients. The United States has developed a special form of Freemasonry, named Prince Hall

Freemasonry after one of its founding members, which is a Masonic organization predominantly for African-American men, its very existence seemingly indicating a deep, cultural apartheid in American Masonry. Grand Lodges may maintain relationships with other Grand Lodges, or they may even formally break off those relationships. Practices are similar in the various jurisdictions, but there is no overall body either to ensure conformity or to speak for all. No one can say with authority that any practice or belief belongs to all Freemasons. No one truly knows all there is to be known about Freemasonry because there is not a single organization which is the Freemasons.

An even greater complexity in understanding Masonic organizations is the concept of appendant bodies. These are societies which recruit solely from within the ranks of Freemasons—or Druids, or any other Masonic organization. You have to be a Freemason before you can apply to join. They are societies within societies. And while the Freemasons might well be a society with secrets (rather than a secret society) some of the appendant bodies do seem to be truly secret societies.

The best known of the appendant bodies is the Scottish Rite, which includes many of the strange rituals and conventions painfully purged from the mainstream of Freemasonry. In order to be a member it is necessary first to have passed through the three degrees of Freemasonry—therefore to be a Master Mason. Scottish Rite offers a further thirty grades of Masonic membership. This is the organization which is the plot device for Dan Brown's *The Lost Symbol*, and while the members he describes are by necessity Freemasons their role in the book is as members of the Scottish Rite appendant body. This may be regarded as an elite group of Freemasons, and if there are secrets within the Masonic organizations maybe those secrets are found somewhere here. For most Scottish Rite freemasons the effective limit of their progress is the thirty-second degree. There is however a thirty-third degree, by invitation only, therefore for the elite of the elite. Scottish Rite has two Grand Lodges in America and one in Britain, and as with the Grand Lodges of the Freemasons there seems to be no overall control.

It can be seen therefore that within the *Alice in Wonderland* Masonic world there can be societies alongside societies, societies within societies. There are different Masonic organizations, a bewildering complexity of national and state jurisdictions, lodges for (mainly) black Americans and those for (mainly) white Americans, numerous appendant bodies, different jurisdictions for the appendant bodies, and even bodies appendant to the appendant bodies. The metaphor is the onion—peel back one layer and there is another layer inside.

Once those curious about Masonry feel they have a grip on the many layers, then it is time to consider the non-Masonic organizations which nonetheless resemble the

Freemasons. For example in Ireland the Orange Order resembles the Freemasons in structures yet maintains no formal links with Masonic groups, nor is it an appendant body. Yet in a parallel with the Scottish Rite appendant to Freemasonry, appendant to the Orange Order is the Royal Black. While Freemasons have the aim of making good men better the Orange Order has a religious, social and political agenda. This agenda has been pursued effectively: the Orange Order has undoubtedly done much to maintain the protestant faith in Ireland, to create a sense of identity among the protestant community, and to campaign for the politics of union with the United Kingdom. The suggestion is that Masonic structures such as those of the Freemasons can easily be put to other uses, and the potential for Freemasons acting in such ways must exist. In *The Lost Symbol* the concept of Masons having a political agenda is skirted. That they may have such an agenda, or may be used by outsiders who have such an agenda, is what makes the Masons potentially concerning.

The Case Against the Masons

Our generation has become concerned about Masons. Once Freemasons were seen simply as the pillars of society, and were given respect purely for being Freemasons. Today the world is less sure of its view of Freemasons and of all Masonic groups.

The case against Freemasons has been made many times, probably most strongly in Stephen Knight's best-seller *The Brotherhood* (1984). The Freemasons themselves ensured this book's success by asking its members not to read it, an action of breathtaking stupidity in an open society. (The Roman Catholic Church similarly instructed its members not to read *The Da Vinci Code* and *Angels and Demons*, and seems to have generated more sales for Dan Brown in the process.) Stephen Knight doesn't like Freemasons, and it shows both in *The Brotherhood* and also in his *Jack the Ripper: The Final Solution*, where he puts forward the view that Jack the Ripper was enacting a series of Masonic ritual killings. He does advance some serious objections to Freemasons, and his key points merit serious consideration. Key objections (from Knight and elsewhere) are:

3. That the Freemasons are a religion, and that they are Satanic. Knight's argument is in my view untenable. That Masonic ritual resembles Christian liturgy and contains numerous Bible references is undoubtedly true, but this only means that the people who wrote the Masonic rituals were familiar with Christian liturgy and the Bible and chose to incorporate elements. Knight's most critical argument is that in the Royal Arch appendant degree the name of God is revealed as the name *Jah-bul-on*, an ugly, composite word of dubious meaning.
4. That Masonic ritual gives cause for concern because of the grizzly oaths which are part of it.

James V:12 gives clear direction against swearing oaths, advice which is followed literally by some Christians (for example Quakers). Very many, Christians and non-Christians, feel shocked by the extreme blood and gore of many of the Masonic oaths. It is hard to escape an implication that if a member of the Masons breaks his vows then the ghastly punishments described will be carried out by other Masons. This is not the intent, but it is the implication. In *The Lost Symbol* this is presented as one of the "bad bits" of Freemasonry. Implicitly Dan Brown has thrown down the challenge to Freemasons today: reform these ghastly oaths. The revisions to ritual of the nineteenth century show that Masonry is in fact able to change its rituals (though members specifically swear not to allow changes)—Freemasonry today needs to go through a process to remove the "bad bits". In Dan Brown's terms (and perhaps also in the terms of the Freemasons themselves) in allowing these abhorrent oaths to continue as part of its rituals, Freemasonry is confusing a symbol of Freemasonry with the core values.

5. Freemasonry today is associated with the idea of a group of people who support and help one another, by implication to the detriment of others who are not Freemasons. The concept is linked with handshakes as a means of recognition (in popular culture "dodgy handshakes") and an

awareness of very high levels of Masonic membership within some professions including the police, the legal profession and the civil service. Within an open society it is hard to find an argument to defend the existence of a society which includes this overt self-help element. Probably a Masonic response would be that this is not what Freemasonry is about, but it is nonetheless how it is perceived.

6. Secret membership lists are no longer acceptable. Within living memory it was right and proper for Freemasons to keep their membership secret. The Nazi persecution of Freemasons in the 1930s and the subsequent murder of many thousands in the holocaust demonstrated the need for such secrecy. But we no longer live in such times. The biggest secret the Freemasons have today is their membership lists, both historic and present, and this is the secret they need to work towards divulging. *The Lost Symbol* raises a tenable scenario where such a membership list suddenly enters the public domain and is a threat to American national security. The solution is surely to be found in managed release of data.

A most serious objection to Freemasons comes through the "P2 Affair". The story is that a lodge of Freemasons was infiltrated by an outside group, possibly the KGB, and came within a hair's breadth of installing a communist government in Italy. The episode chimes with Dan Brown's plot device of the Scottish Rite Masons infiltrated by Mal'akh.

P2 is the Italian Masonic lodge "Propaganda Due", which in fairness it should be pointed out has nothing to do with British or American Freemasonry, though its structures are essentially the same. P2 was established in 1966, and from 1969 had Licio Gelli as its Venerable Master. Gelli's modus operandi was nothing other than blackmail. Taking its membership from the Italian elite it demanded as Masonic dues not money but secrets, using these to blackmail both existing members and people whom P2 wanted to recruit. Ultimately in 1981 the Italian authorities raided Gelli's home in Milan, and while they found Gelli had fled the country in advance of the raid they did recover membership lists for P2 (which some believe were deliberately left for them to find). In a list of around a thousand names, all linked with fraudulent activity and all having given a personal oath of loyalty to Gelli, they found:

- three Cabinet ministers
- several former prime ministers (some dispute on the exact number).
- 43 MPs representing all main political parties, except the Communists.
- 54 top civil servants.
- 8 admirals including the commander of the armed forces.
- 30 generals.

- 19 judges.
- the editor of Italy's leading newspaper *Il Corriere Della Sera.*
- directors of all of the three Italian intelligence services.
- lawyers, magistrates, police chiefs, professors, political party leaders.

The immediate result was the fall of the government. It seemed likely that the only party not implicated—the Communists—would form the next government, with clearly expressed pro-Soviet sympathies. The argument is plausible that Gelli deliberately left behind when he fled the names only of non-Communist party members in order to bring about precisely this result. In the event the Communists did not form a government—rather Italy managed a most unlikely five-party coalition brokered by their 85-year old President, Alessandro Pertini.

The P2 affair also enters the murky waters of the murder of Robert Calvi, the chairman of the Vatican owned Banco Ambrosiano popularly known as "God's Banker". He was a member of P2. Conspiracy theorists have gone to town with ideas that Banco Ambrosiano was laundering money for the Mafia and for P2, and that P2 was in effect running the finances of the Vatican. Dig deep enough and you can find conspiracy theorists who believe that Pope John Paul I found this out, and that his death in 1978 after just a month as pope was in fact a murder by P2 to silence him. Conspiracy theorists see the murder of Calvi as being by P2 because Calvi was going to reveal them, and that his murder was carried out in a ritualistic way that would intimidate other P2 members—he was found hung beneath Blackfriars Bridge in London. The story of Calvi's death puts on trial the whole concept of Masonry. Whether the conspiracy theories are right or not hardly matters; rather the conspiracy theories around Calvi's death present a scenario of how a Masonic lodge might go wrong and stoop to the murder of a pope and a banker. The story doesn't have to be true to be a cause for concern; rather it just needs to be credible. Against the backdrop of the very many successful prosecutions of P2 members we have to accept that P2 has been proved to have been a real threat to Italy. This is Masonry at its worst.

In Dan Brown's world the Masons are in effect shown to run the world. In the example of P2 we have the structure of a Masonic lodge (albeit an Italian one not recognized by British or American lodges) being used to bring down a government, end the careers of approaching a thousand senior people and almost succeeding in installing a pro-Soviet Communist government in Italy. The worry is indeed infiltration of the Freemasons. Dan Brown touches only obliquely on the concept of infiltration—Mal'akh is indeed an infiltrator, but he is just one man, does not become a Grand Master and does not control a lodge. Yet the story of P2 shows that infiltration can turn a lodge into a weapon. Freemasonry with its secret membership lists has the potential to be used for evil.

The Case For the Masons

It is easy to criticize the Masons and therefore easy to forget the strong case for them.

At its simplest the case in favour is to look at their achievement. In Christian terms this is expressed in Luke's gospel:

> There is no such thing as a good tree producing worthless fruit, nor yet a worthless tree producing good fruit. For each tree is known by its own fruit: you do not gather figs from thistles, and you do not pick grapes from brambles. A good man produces good from the store of good within himself; and an evil man from evil within produces evil.
>
> *Luke* VI:43-45

The vine should be judged by the fruit, and in every area of society Freemasons do indeed produce good fruit. Most Freemasons, most of the time, are good men. The idea that Freemasonry takes good men and seeks to make them better does indeed seem to be a part of the reality. In *The Lost Symbol* we see Freemasons who are good people trying to do the right thing.

Masonic practice contains much within it which seems strange, but also has parts which have a beauty and power that is breathtaking. Consider for example the well known Biblical description of the virtues: "And now faith, hope, and love abide, these three; and the greatest of these is love" *1 Corinthians* XIII:13. The Masonic second degree lecture includes a most remarkable passage which serves as a reflection on this theme:

> The ladder which Jacob saw in his vision extended from earth to heaven, and the principal rounds were denominated Faith, Hope and Charity which admonish us to have Faith in the Grand Architect, Hope in immortality and Charity to all mankind. The greatest of these is Charity. For our Faith may be lost in sight, Hope may end in fruition, but Charity extends beyond the grave through the boundless realms of eternity.

What is the Secret of the Masons?

Indeed do the Freemasons or any other group of Masons have a secret?

The Freemasons have traditionally guarded the text of their rituals, so for a couple of centuries the rituals themselves were indeed a secret. Today those rituals are published (though not by the Freemasons) and we can all see the secrets contained. They are no longer a secret.

And anyway, as secrets go they are a damp squib! They are best regarded as moral, allegorical texts. Much in them is opaque, and it is hard to escape the view that for the majority of Freemasons they are little better than gibberish. Probably the easiest way to understand them is to see them as a creation in the seventeenth century or earlier reflecting the language and theological concerns of that time, but including within them some reworked earlier material including mediaeval texts. As such they are not a secret. If there is a secret at all it is in the form of something hidden behind these texts. It is (just) within the bounds of possibility that they refer back to early Christian or Judaic writings now lost and that they may contain a confused echo of stories and moral teaching within the Judaeo-Christian tradition but not part of the scriptural cannon of either. For example the building of Solomon's Temple is only briefly described in the Old Testament yet this story is told at length by Masonic ritual. Probably this reflects the imagination of a ritual writer; just possibly it truly reflects a tradition or a text otherwise lost. Whatever the ritual might mean, there seems to be no-one in Craft Freemasonry today competent to give an authoritative, evidenced interpretation. If the rituals themselves do represent some secret then the Freemasons have guarded it so well that they have forgotten it themselves!

The true secret of Freemasonry today is its membership lists. In public life it is a requirement that all declare whatever interests they might have. Freemasonry is exceptional in that it has a secret membership, with members discouraged from revealing their membership, and bound to one another and to secrecy by oaths. The UK has recently seen the media circus created by the leak to a newspaper of details of the expenses claimed by MPs. This is as nothing to the media frenzy that would be created by access to Freemasons' membership records, so that we could see in all walks of life that people who claimed to be independent of one another were operating within the fraternal bonds of Freemasonry. The membership lists are dynamite. Arguably the requirements of democracy and a free society are that they should be made public, yet there is scant chance of this happening. This is the big, guarded secret.

Accessed through Freemasonry are the appendant Masonic organizations, including for example the Scottish Rite. Much of their ritual is still secret, and it is within the bounds of possibility that something within this ritual might be of scholarly interest and might even be kept secret for a reason. It is within the bounds of belief (just!) that groups including the Knights Templar may have come into contact with early Masonic groups. Just possibly some information is locked away within the vaults of say the Scots Rite. But as with the Freemasons it is the membership list which is the true secret.

The sort of mindset that is happy with an organization within an organization—say a Scots Rite within Freemasonry—could conceive of yet another layer to the onion. By this logic there should be an elite organization within Scots Rite itself, a society that really and truly is secret.

Masonic Structures

The basic unit of Freemasonry is the Lodge. This is a local gathering of Freemasons around a building or set of rooms which constitutes the regular meeting place of that particular lodge.

Every Lodge should be subordinate to a Grand Lodge. The oldest is the United Grand Lodge of England. There is a Grand Lodge for Ireland and a Grand Lodge for Scotland. In America each state has its own Grand Lodge. On the European Continent there are typically Grand Lodges for units smaller than countries, frequently called Grand Orients. Typically Grand Lodges recognize one another so that freemasons within one system are welcomed at lodges in the other systems, though there is no over-arching organization which links freemasonry worldwide.

The structure has flexibility, but also may be problematic:

- It is possible to have a Lodge which is not recognised by a Grand Lodge, for example Lodges that were set up by prisoners of war during the Second World War. Such an "irregular" Lodge may or may not keep to the norms of Freemasonry. In any event it is without the control and guidance of a Grand Lodge.
- A Lodge in dispute with a Grand Lodge may become irregular, and therefore operate without any overall control or guidance.
- At one time most jurisdictions had two different and competing rites of Freemasonry, called Antient and Modern, and therefore both Antient and Modern Grand Lodges. These differences have now been resolved, though the heritage of the Antient/Modern split affects the present characteristics of Grand Lodges.

- The lack of an overall controlling body means that Freemasonry has developed in different ways in different countries. In particular the British and American tradition has formally cut its ties with the Continental tradition.
- It is not necessary for a Lodge to be recognised by its national or state Grand Lodge. In America there are Lodges comprising primarily African-American men (the Prince Hall Lodges) which developed independently from the state Grand Lodges of the USA and which are instead recognised by the United Grand Lodge of England.

The structure means that it is very hard to complete sentences starting "Freemasonry is ..." or "Freemasons believe ..." The reality is that there are differences between different jurisdictions, and even between individual Lodges.

A great complicating factor in looking at the structures of Freemasonry is the existence of the many appendant bodies. These include the following large groups:

- Scottish Rite
- York Rite
- Order of the Eastern Star
- Order of the Amaranth

These and many others are Masonic but they are not strictly Freemasons. The complexity they exhibit is bewildering.

Then there are organizations which exist on Masonic lines, but have no direct affiliation with a Grand Lodge. Such are legion! Often many members are also Freemasons. The Orange Order in Ireland is in structure thoroughly Masonic, though is not recognized by a Grand Lodge. Likewise the Order of Pythias (mainly in America) and the Oddfellows (formed in Britain but with offshoots in America) may reasonably be regarded as Masonic, but are not Freemasons. The vast majority of the Greek fraternities at US Universities are Masonic, as are many of the US student societies (including the Skull and Bones at Yale).

The metaphor often used is that of the layers of an onion. A member of a Lodge may progress through the three degrees of membership offered by Freemasonry, at each stage entering deeper into the allegorical and esoteric life of the Freemasons. However on completing the third degree—the third layer of the onion—he finds there are other Masonic organizations available. For example the Scottish Rite offers thirty more layers of the onion, leading to a thirty third degree. This is not Freemasonry, but it is Masonry.

One of the most concerning organizations on Masonic lines is Yale University's **Skull and Bones** society. Every year fifteen students at Yale University join Skull and Bones—an organization which may be the world's most powerful society.

These "Bonesmen"—and since 1991 "Boneswomen" as well—belong to a society whose symbol is a skull and crossed bones over the number 322, and who meet in an austerely designed building nicknamed "The Tomb". Quite what they get up to is a matter of speculation but this is more than a student glee club. Both presidents Bush were members, as was Senator John Kenny (who ran against George W Bush in 2004), and a long list of the great and the good in American society.

The society cannot properly be called secret. Basically everyone knows about it. We know where the society's premises are and the names of most of their members. Indeed rather than being a secret society, Skull and Bones is now probably the best known of all the US student societies. It has even entered into popular culture. In *The Simpsons* bad guy Montgomery Burns is described as a Bonesman, while Skull and Bones make it into the Doonesbury comic strips and the 2006 film *The Good Shepherd*. What is secret is not its existence, but what its members do, and here we have to admit we know very little.

Skull and Bones was founded in 1832. Quite why it has a skull and crossed bones as its symbol is not clear, nor is the meaning of the number 322 . The idea has been put forward that 322 refers to the death date of Demosthenes, and that the society asserts some sort of lineage back to 322—an idea surely wholly implausible. It has been suggested that the 32 means 1832, the foundation year, and the 2 means 2nd lodge—suggesting that somewhere out there is a truly secret Skull and Bones 1st lodge, and perhaps even a secret 3rd lodge, all three founded in the year '32. Over the years there have been a few events around Skull and Bones that have received media interest, particularly the contested decision to admit women, though the overall sense is that the society has largely remained beneath the radar screen and been happy so to do.

Every spring fifteen new members join Skull and Bones, all junior year students at Yale University. The process is called "tapping", but quite why a decision is made to "tap" someone is not clear, though there seems to be predisposition towards recruiting from the ranks of some other Yale groups. For example the Yale fraternity Delta Kappa Epsilon, itself the student home of five of America's 43 presidents, is effectively a conduit for Skull and Bones members, as are Yale Political Union and Yale Daily News. Once admitted members meet twice a week. The stated goal is to develop friendship and connections with fellow members, and to explore ideas leading to personal growth.

The more plausible stories about Skull and Bones include the following:

- The society is an aristocratic elite. Certain New England families occur again and again as its members, and these families are frequently intermarried.
- Initiation is through a ritual similar to some Masonic ceremonies. The initiate is placed in a coffin.

- Pranks by members include thefts of objects. Members call this process "crooking" and the intention is to "crook" the most outrageous item. The process creates a bond between members.
- Members are required to exchange intimate details of their sexual histories, thus creating a bond between them.
- Extensive use is made of nicknames.
- The society has been accused of stealing and retaining skulls, including those of US president Martin Van Buren, Apache leader Geronimo and Mexican revolutionary general Pancho Villa.
- Throughout their lives the society's members occupy leading positions in the US and support one another in promoting the values of the society. Today there are about 600 members alive.

The more extreme stories about Skull and Bones include the following:

- Once initiated there is no way out.
- Members know the society by the name "Brotherhood of Death".
- They recruit exclusively white Anglo-Saxon protestants, with purely token exceptions in recent years.
- George Bush (senior) was a Skull and Bones project, with his career promoted at every stage by Skull and Bones. Ditto his son George W Bush.

- The CIA is effectively run by Skull and Bones.
- They seek a New World Order where the USA controls the world, and seek to crush any opposition to US world control, whether it comes from enemies (eg during the cold war the USSR) or allies (the UK).
- They believe in "constructive chaos" in order to promote US interests. This includes a destabilised Middle East.
- Goals are to be met through a policy of ambiguity and deceit. Bonesmen are only ever truly loyal to other bonesmen. The elite 600 or so truly rules America from behind the scenes, whether the president is a Republican or a Democrat.
- The intellectual foundations of Skull and Bones include some uncompromising right-wing views.
- The vaults of the Skull and Bones contains some of Hitler's war loot.
- The nineteenth century society had members involved in drug running—indeed its founder was an opium smuggler.

All the above can be found in a five minute internet search, and do not represent my views or opinions. Rather they are ideas which are out there, with varying degrees of supporting evidence. What does seem clear is that Skull and Bones is enormously powerful, and that its goals are not published. It may be that the primary allegiance of

Skull and Bones members is to their society, not to their family, church or country.

Items of Interest

The Masonic name for God—**Jahbulon**—has caused much concern and is central to Knight's contention that the Masons are Satanic. The name occurs in the Royal Arch side degree (an adjunct to the third degree) and is not actually part of the mainstream of Freemasonry. However as a philologist (with a PhD in the subject) I find the arguments advanced around this name fascinating and I venture a brief digression on the topic.

Jahbulon is explained by Royal Arch Masons as a composite word of three parts:

- Jah is Yehovah, the God of the Old Testament
- Bul is Baal, the false god that the Israelites for a time worshipped and who was later associated with the devil.
- On is Osiris, an Egyptian deity, by some seen as a prefigure of Christ (a man whose life foretold the coming of Christ), by some (including John Milton in Paradise Lost, one of Dan Brown's sources) as a devil.

Many are (understandably) deeply unhappy by this ugly, composite name which appears to fuse God and the devil as if the two are equivalent. My thought—from the discipline of philology—is that the explanation offered for this name by Masons is philologically untenable. Whatever its origin it is not what they argue. Specifically:

- Language rarely functions by taking three proper nouns and sticking them together. I cannot bring to mind a single comparable case.
- Jah- only superficially resembles Jehovah. At best it is the first syllable of Yahweh (though Masons claim Jehovah).
- Bul as a form of Baal is most unlikely. Vowels do change a lot in languages. A change of a long lower back vowel –aa- to the long top back vowel –uu- is a major one and needs a reason. Jahbalon rolls off the tongue more easily.
- On cannot possibly be Osiris. Nasals (like the –n) don't spontaneously appear.

If the three names Jehovah, Baal and Osiris were to be put together (not that languages usually do this) the expected form would be Jebaalos. I cannot imagine what Jahbulon might be, but it I'm convinced it is something else. I think we are seeing a form whose meaning has become forgotten and which has been "explained" by someone with a false etymology. Possibly the thinking behind the explanation was that the devil—baal—is linguistically imprisoned between God the father, Jehovah, and Osiris as a name for Christ, though this is bad philology and dubious theology. Intriguingly the form Jahbulon looks as if it should be capable of a proper interpretation.

10. THE MAN WHO WROTE *THE LOST SYMBOL*

Dan Brown has not sought publicity, and those who have sought to find out something about the man behind the books have found it something of a work of extrapolation from surprisingly thin pieces of evidence. Dan Brown could make life easier for all critics by publishing a biography.

Meeting the Deadline

It seems that meeting deadlines is not Dan Brown's strongest feature. *The Lost Symbol* was expected in 2006 and presumably started in 2004. The publication date was pushed back several times, with it finally appearing on September 15, 2009. An effort has been made to rationalize the publication date as 09-15-09 which written 09+15+09 equals 33. I don't believe it for a minute! Rather Dan Brown seems to have had a serious case of writer's block. Furthermore his book does not seem to have had the minute proof reading that a book selling the millions of copies of this title might expect. A plausible scenario seems to be that Dan Brown got the final manuscript to his publisher a few days after the absolutely last deadline for the revised publication date and the editorial proof reading has missed some issues.

Dan Brown reports that he gets up at 4am. Personally I'm not sure that clocks in my home even display the time 4am, but if he gets up at this ghastly hour he must have plenty of time at his disposal for writing. If he wrote a page before breakfast he would have it written within a couple of years. In fact most authors reckon they need to publish at least a book a year to survive, and most authors would find that their publishers would not tolerate a three year delay. Clearly Dan Brown is not most authors. His output is not large. Perhaps quality is more important than quantity.

Realistically the phenomenal success of previous books must have had an impact on his writing. The simplest impact is that it takes away the need to write in order to earn a living. Dan Brown doesn't actually have to write another word ever again in order to live very comfortably. But I suggest there is a more complex impact that comes with success: responsibility. *The Da Vinci Code* has sold around 80 million copies to date and has been read by maybe twice that number of people. This is an enormous impact, and with it comes an awareness that what you write really matters. For example had Dan Brown chosen in *The Lost Symbol* to condemn the Masons he could have done real damage to Masonry worldwide. Instead he has been broadly supportive. In *The Lost Symbol* Dan Brown has put forward a mystical religious view which is important and which he needed to get this right, and if it took an extra three years I guess we all had to be patient for a very good reason.

The Man and the Book

What are the influences in the life of Dan Brown which have enabled him to write *The Lost Symbol*? Dan Brown has sought to preserve his privacy, and details of his life in the public domain are frustratingly scant. Indeed enough puzzles remain to give conspiracy theorists ample scope.

Daniel Gerhard Brown was born 22nd June 1964 in the small town of Exeter, New Hampshire, the town in which he still lives. His father Richard Brown was math teacher at the prestigious Phillips Exeter Academy. As a new faculty member he lived, with his wife Connie, in the dorms of Phillips Exeter Academy, and it was here that Dan Brown spent his earliest years.

The Brown family were committed members of Christ Church, the Episcopalian church in Exeter—Connie Brown was organist there, and both Richard and Connie directed the choir. This is the sort of world which we see in *The Lost Symbol* as Washington Cathedral and in which milieu Colin Galloway fits. The Episcopal Church was a formative influence for Dan Brown. Even when the Brown family moved out of the Academy dorms—about 1975—they moved to a home which was just a few yards from Christ Church. Indeed their home was built on a site which had once been designated for the Christ Church rectory. Christ Church was central to the lives of the whole family, with Dan Brown singing in the choir there, going to Sunday School, and attending Church Camp. By this time the Brown family comprised three children—Dan the eldest, his sister Valerie Jo (born 1966) and his brother Gregory (born 1974). Presumably life in the Academy dorms had become a little cramped with three children; certainly Richard Brown had more than fulfilled the ten years of residence in dorms expected of young faculty members.

Dan Brown (and in their turn his sister and brother) attended first an elementary school in Exeter, then Phillips Exeter Academy, graduating in 1982. Though once a boys' school, the Academy had in 1970 begun to admit girls also. By the time that Dan Brown was a pupil there it was fully co-educational. Religion was central to the Academy, with a daily religious service ecumenical in character and inclusive of many Christian groups as well as to Jewish and Buddhist believers. A spirit of religious tolerance is evident, and again this seems to be picked up in *The Lost Symbol*, where many religions are seen as vehicles for the same fundamental truths, the Ancient Mysteries. The Academy also has a remarkably large library in an award-winning building. Taking both borders and day pupils the Academy faced the inevitable split engendered by these two very different categories. While at the school Dan Brown was a day pupil as his parents lived locally, though his childhood experience of living in the dorms and his parents' many links with the school may have gone some way to bridge the divide.

The excellent academic foundations of Phillips Exeter Academy prepare many of its alumni for places in Ivy League universities: Harvard, Yale, Princeton, Dartmouth, University of Pennsylvania, Columbia, Cornell, and Brown. About a third of graduates in any year go on to one of these most prestigious of US universities, a school achievement which is truly outstanding. Others choose the smaller colleges of the "Little Ivy League". Dan Brown selected one of these, Amherst College. In 2004 Amherst admitted 400 freshmen from an application pool of well over 5,000, a statistic which demonstrates that the quality of this small college is every bit as high as the bigger universities of the Ivy League—indeed Amherst appears in second place in current league tables of US liberal arts colleges. Amherst College is a two hour drive from Exeter, and it may well be that Dan Brown was comfortable living at a College in this proximity to his home town. Langdon is of course a Harvard professor, not an Amherst professor, but we should probably see Langdon as modeled on a type of professor Dan Brown indeed saw at Amherst. He seems to have recognized the international fame of Harvard in linking his hero with this university rather than the similarly excellent though much smaller and therefore less well known Amherst.

At Amherst Dan Brown took a combined major in English and Spanish, a syllabus that included a broad introduction to the Arts. At the time when Dan Brown started at Amherst the college had a fully functioning "Greek" fraternity system where on campus accommodation and social life was dominated by these student societies. In 1983 Dan Brown joined Psi Upsilon. Most of his male peers would have joined one fraternity or another. This is Dan Brown's personal experience of a Masonic style organization, and probably his only experience, as no one seems to have linked him with the Freemasons or any other Masonic group.

Though a long-established part of Amherst life the fraternity system was at that time under attack. Amherst had once been a men-only college, but had admitted women from 1976. Yet the fraternities remained men only, with the fraternities controlling such perks as on-campus housing. Clearly this wasn't equitable, and the authorities had to intervene. The College acted in 1983—shortly after Dan Brown had joined—by banning the fraternities from on-campus activities.

Quite what happened subsequently is open to speculation from conspiracy theorists. Today Psi Upsilon does exist at Amherst as an off-campus fraternity admitting women and men—exactly what Amherst College wanted. Yet this approved fraternity seems very different from the original Psi Upsilon—arguably it is a neutered version of the old fraternity. Students didn't accept the change without complaint, for in 1983 there were many members of Psi Upsilon (and of other Amherst fraternities) who were less than happy with the changes imposed by the College. While many members complied with the College rules, others left the fraternities and some formed secret fraternities, so it is thought that there was a secret (men only) Psi Upsilon alongside the College approved co-educational fraternity. In 1983 the choice for men was either to be part of the fraternities as revised by their college, join a secret fraternity which preserved the male-only status and traditions of the old system, do both, or indeed leave the fraternity system completely. Dan Brown's decision is not known.

The fraternity system is in many respects Masonic, often conceived in part as a life-long self-help organization. It has a framework which naturally lends itself to secrecy. The action of Amherst College had as an unintended consequence the creation of secret fraternities, a consequence which could reasonably be anticipated and which may explain their seven year delay between admitting women and acting to end on-campus discrimination against women. In a sense the cure was as bad as the problem. Dan Brown has at least seen at first hand the sort of problems that can beset organizations structured on Masonic lines.

In addition to his fraternity membership, at Amherst Dan Brown was a part of the Amherst College Glee Club. Despite the associations its name may conjure up, this is a very staid body, offering high quality musical performances. Dan Brown was a choir member, part of the bass section, and took part in the Glee Club's 1983 world tour: Paris, Venice, Vienna, Athens, Delhi, Tokyo, Taipei, Hong Kong, Seoul. Along with time in Spain as part of his studies Dan Brown had an introduction to the cities of Europe and Asia. While he clearly travelled both as a student and subsequently he is not the sort of globe-trotter he portrays in Langdon.

Music was clearly Dan Brown's passion, and on leaving Amherst College he moved to Los Angeles with the intention of launching a musical career. This is hardly the career move expected from a young man who has benefited from one of the best and most expensive educations that America can offer. He certainly recorded music—*SynthAnimals* (1989) and *Perspective* (1990) were both self-produced—though nothing that made his fame or fortune. He worked for a time as a counselor for "The Millionaires Club", a Los Angeles singles club (a job he may be imagined to have obtained through Amherst connections), and for a time as an English Literature teacher at a Beverley Hills preparatory school. Presumably neither job paid the bills. Around 1991 he secured some support from the National Academy of Songwriters to act as his agent.

The "Director of Artistic Development" at the National Academy of Songwriters was Blythe Newlon. She worked hard to promote Dan Brown, and though twelve years his senior in time became his wife.

As a musician Dan Brown is competent. He knows how to sing, and has a good voice. But he does not have a unique voice, nor did he try to market any songs which are in themselves remarkable. He is pleasing to listen to, but unmemorable. As a musician Dan Brown was not going to make it. He moved back to Exeter in 1993—with Blythe

Newlon—and there produced his final CD with the title *Angels and Demons*—a title he of course re-used as that of one of his novels. Yet the CD did not sell well, and it is perhaps at this time that Dan Brown began to accept that he was not going to be able to make a career as a musician pay. His novel writing is in effect a second career, and may even have been born out of desperation. On his website he says that his inspiration was reading the novel *Doomsday Conspiracy* by Sidney Sheldon while on holiday in Tahiti around 1993 and thinking "Hey, I can do that".

The mid 1990s may well have been difficult years for Dan Brown. He did some English Literature teaching at Phillips Exeter Academy, though not as a faculty member, and also taught at nearby Stratham. When his engagement to Blythe Newsom was announced in 1996 she was described as a dental technician. Following their marriage Dan Brown published two humorous books, which did not sell well. *187 Men to Avoid* (1997) is under the nom de plume Danielle Brown and lists 187 characteristics of men that should cause women to avoid them. *The Bald Book* (1998) followed, in the name of Blythe Brown though with Dan Brown listed as the copyright owner and presumed author. Around this time Dan Brown was working on his first novel. While it may well have been conceived as early as 1993 the writing and publication process took around five years. The first publisher that saw it accepted it, which may reflect the quality of Dan Brown's writing, or more likely may reflect a mistake where he did not secure a sufficiently prestigious publisher.

Digital Fortress was published in 1998 by Thomas Dunne Books, an imprint of St Martin's Press—and fizzled. It followed the path of most novels. Though competently written and receiving some positive reviews it did not reach the ranks of a novel which bookshops were prepared to give much space to. Thomas Dunne Books probably lacked the market reach to promote the book to the extent the author would have liked. *Digital Fortress* therefore saw a few months of modest sales followed by a slip into obscurity, which in the ordinary course of events is where it would be still.

It is common for publishers of fiction to offer contracts for the first three of an author's books, so that if the author writes a best-seller they are tied to the original publisher for the sequel. Probably Dan Brown had this sort of agreement with Thomas Dunne Books. His second novel, *Angels and Demons* (2000) performed well, and it may well be that Dan Brown was reluctant to offer a third to the same small publisher. Indeed his decision to stay with Thomas Dunne Books for his third novel is only really explicable if there was some sort of contractual tie in, for this publisher is not of the size to market a book that sells well to its best potential.

Deception Point (2001) is a well-written novel. Yet it leaves the character of Robert Langdon, developed in *Angels and Demons*, and introduces a new hero. The idea that Dan

Brown wrote a novel to satisfy his contractual obligation to a publisher is persuasive. From a creative point of view it does seem to be something of a dead end.

The Da Vinci Code (2003) is the novel that truly made Dan Brown famous. Published by Doubleday Group (in the United States) and Bantam Books (in the United Kingdom) it benefits from two publishers who have the market penetration to make the book a true bestseller. And bestseller it indeed is, with sales of 80 million worldwide, and translations into 44 languages. It is this book (and this book alone) that made Dan Brown's name, though *Angels and Demons* had shown promise. The renewed popularity of the earlier Dan Brown novels has been subsequent to the publication of *The Da Vinci Code*.

I expect the next Dan Brown novel three to six years after publication of *The Lost Symbol* (so 2012-2015). I would be thrilled to see a novel sooner, but I see no early signs. *The Da Vinci Code* contained a coded message referring to the next book. There is nothing like this in *The Lost Symbol*. Possibly this means that Dan Brown hasn't yet decided just what the plot of the next book will be. Or perhaps he just likes to keep us all guessing!

The Conspiracy Theories

Is there a secret in Dan Brown's life? There are indeed puzzles:

- How did a relatively undistinguished writer get the marketing support to make *The Da Vinci Code* such a runaway best seller? This is a remarkable state of affairs and the idea sometimes proposed that it can be explained simply by his wife's support sounds weak. Most books don't get anything like the level of marketing support this book received—however hard a spouse lobbies!
- Why was *The Lost Symbol* so late being published? Did Dan Brown feel the need to wait until after the end of the Bush presidency? Or is he just bad at meeting deadlines?
- Why has Dan Brown not told his fans a little more about his life? Is there really something he wants to hide?
- Robert Langdon (who is modelled on Dan Brown) seems aware of an alternative world history, involving the Priory of Sion, Templars, Illuminati, Freemasons and lots more. If such an alternative history is credible (a big if) Amherst is just the sort of place where serious academic research in this difficult area may be done. Is Dan Brown publishing as fiction something discovered by scholars at Amherst and which is too controversial or dangerous for them to publish as fact?
- A conspiracy theorist could argue that Dan Brown is the protégé of a secret version of Amherst's Psi Upsilon fraternity and is being used as a

> mouthpiece to propose ideas they want to see discussed, but which no academic is ever going to put forward. This suggests that the assumed clandestine Psi Upsilon has an intellectual agenda

Taken together there are some surprises in Dan Brown's life in the form of events that really don't add up. Whether these truly add up to grounds for a conspiracy theory is another matter entirely. As a product of America's professional class, a graduate of Phillips Exeter Academy and Amherst College, he is well placed to access the networks and privileges which exist—people of his social class do have interesting and successful lives. His efforts to establish a Hollywood career must surely have been supported by his parents' money. The casual jobs he obtained are not the ordinary lowly-skilled hourly-paid work but rather speak of connections. For example it is hard to see what qualification Dan Brown had to be a singles' counselor. While he was qualified to teach English and Spanish (in as much as he had a BA degree in these subjects) his employment with prestigious Phillips Exeter Academy suggests recommendation by a contact, presumably his father. He has been persistent in seeking a creative career. His initial musical efforts were self produced and therefore presumably self funded, while his later musical efforts would have generated only a minimal income. His humor books did little or nothing—though as he must have known before writing them the genre is not one that tends to produce best-sellers. His novel writing career has not been prolific. Indeed since he decided on writing in 1993 he has in sixteen years produced five books, roughly three years a book. This is way below the received wisdom that a novelist needs to write a book a year in order to make a living. It may possibly be little more than a fluke that Dan Brown got his big break with *The Da Vinci Code*, and that his success is primarily down to luck. He tried hard and repeatedly, and one of his efforts worked. Or it might be something else.

For those determined to find a conspiracy in Dan Brown's life it is surprisingly easy to do so, and conspiracy ideas are fuelled by his reluctance to give interviews talking about his life and inspiration. My own assessment is that it is most likely that Dan Brown was simply in the right place at the right time. He has been tenacious in developing a creative career, and he got some lucky breaks. However I cannot completely put aside the idea that many of the quasi-historical themes in Dan Brown's books are those that serious academics would like to see debated, but which are topics which they feel are too sensational and would damage their career if they themselves put them forward. Maybe there is an academic in the background putting forward many of the ideas in his books—a real Robert Langdon - and maybe there has been a guiding hand promoting Dan Brown as the popularize of these ideas.

11. DAN BROWN'S MESSAGES

In *The Lost Symbol* Dan Brown advances what must be regarded as a theological message. He states all the following:

1. We have a soul that lives after death.
2. That soul should be understood within the context of the "light within", or a "divine spark".
3. After death the soul which comes from God rises up to heaven—to God which is its home—or falls to hell.
4. God is within us all (the message of Luke's gospel).
5. Hell exists and is unimaginably terrible.
6. Prayers are heard. I don't think Dan Brown actually says they are answered, though this is the implicit continuation of the idea.
7. The mind has hidden strengths. Sometimes we understand these as intuition.
8. "On earth as it is in heaven"—or as above, so below. The physical and metaphysical realms are closely linked.
9. Love is the most important thing. Peter Solomon's final message to his dying son Mal'akh is to tell him that he was loved.
10. Human beings are imperfect. Mal'akh strives for a type of perfection and fails.

11. There is truth contained in all the great religions. For Dan Brown the lost symbol is both Jesus Christ and the Bible - whose message is lost because it is rarely understood.
12. The Church—and by extension all organised religion—has lost its way.
13. The new world order of the second coming is very close—and many people who read *The Lost Symbol* will see it. For Dan Brown this is not through a millennium bug or nuclear apocalypse but through the advances of the digital age through which the world truly manages to communicate.
14. There is Ancient Wisdom.

The Masons are presented positively in *The Lost Symbol* because they recognize many and perhaps all of Dan Brown's messages. The United States of America—according to Dan Brown—was created as a way of bringing in the new world order. And according to the plot of the book the revelation of the Masonic Pyramid is a device for advancing Dan Brown's final theological message:

> The Second Coming will be soon, in the lives of many people who read the book.

12. GREAT QUOTES FROM THE LOST SYMBOL

The Lost Symbol has a quality rare among blockbuster novels—it is actually worth quoting. Not all of the good quotes are original Dan Brown, but quite a few are. Those set out below seem to me to be worth reflecting on. It is sentences such as these that lifts *The Lost Symbol* from just another thriller to a book which really has something to say and which can claim to be a serious work of literature.

> To live in the world without becoming aware of the meaning of the world is like wandering around in a great library without touching the books. (Introductory quotation from Manly Palmer Hall's description of his 1928 book *The Secret Teachings of All Ages*)
>
> The secret is how to die. (prologue)
>
> all of the best secrets are hidden in plain view. (chapter 6)
>
> the Masons are not a secret society ... they are a society with secrets. (chapter 6)
>
> Wide acceptance of an idea is not proof of its validity. (chapter 79)
>
> America's intended destiny has been lost to history. (chapter 20)
>
> What happens when those beliefs that we accept on *faith* ... are suddenly categorically proven as *fact*? (chapter 22)
>
> ... how different a world it might be if more leaders took time to ponder the finality of death before racing off to war. (chapter 38)

... most Christians want it both ways. They want to be able proudly to declare that they are believers in the Bible yet simply ignore those parts they find too difficult or too inconvenient to believe. (chapter 49)

I've learned *never* to close my mind to an idea simply because it seems miraculous. (chapter 53)

There are secrets out there that transcend human understanding. (chapter 77)

Is it not possible that we are still living in the Dark Ages? (chapter 82)

Know ye not that ye are gods? (chapter 82; the Hermetic aphorism)

Ye are gods! (chapter 82; *Psalms* LXXXII:6)

Behind the secrets of nature remains something subtle, intangible and inexplicable. (chapter 82; Albert Einstein)

I never imagined that I would live to witness this moment. (chapter 84)

The church had long ago lost her way. (chapter 87)

The kingdom of God is within you. (chapter 102; *Luke* XVII:21—many translations say The kingdom of God is among you)

Know thyself. (chapter 102; Pythagoras)

In this moment, Robert Langdon realized his true insignificance in the universe. (chapter 102)

Can I weigh a human soul? (chapter 107)

Maybe there is a universal truth embedded in everybody's soul. (chapter 111)

We are in the narrow window of time during which we will bear witness to our ultimate renaissance. (chapter 111)

The Apocalypse is coming ... and it will be nothing like what we were taught. (chapter 111)

What we have done for ourselves alone dies with us; what we have done for others and the world remains and is immortal. (chapter 121; Albert Pike)

The works I do, you can do ... and greater (chapter 131, the words of Jesus at *John* XIV:12)

Nothing is hidden that will not be made know; nothing is secret that will not come to light. (epilogue; a synthesis of *Luke* VIII:17, *Luke* XII:2, *Mark* IV:22 and *Matthew* X:26)

13. DAN BROWN BIBLIOGRAPHY

Novels by Dan Brown

Digital Fortress, 1998.

Angels & Demons, 2000.

Deception Point, 2001.

The Da Vinci Code, 2003.

The Lost Symbol, 2009.

The Films

The Da Vinci Code, 2006.

Angels & Demons, 2009.

The Lost Symbol, expected 2012.

Minor Books by Dan Brown

Men to Avoid: A Survival Guide for the Romantically Frustrated Woman, 1995, under the pseudonym Danielle Brown.

The Bald Book, 1998.

Dan Brown's CDs

SynthAnimals, undated (about 1989) and self-produced.

Perspective, 1990, Dalliance.

Dan Brown, 1993, DBG Records.

Angels & Demons, 1994, DBG Records.

Musica Animalia, 2003, Families First charity.

Books about Dan Brown

Boa, Kenneth and Turner, John Alan, *The Gospel According to the Da Vinci Code: The Truth Behind the Writings of Dan Brown,* B&H Publishing Group, 2006.

Brown, D M, *Dan Brown's Road to Success: An Unauthorized Biography of the Creator of the Da Vinci Code,* Lulu Press, 2005.

Cox, Simon, *The Dan Brown Companion,* Random House/Mainstream Publishing, 2006.

Eble, Betsy, *Depth and Details: A Reader's Guide to Dan Brown's 'The Da Vinci Code',* 2004.

Helfers, John (editor), *The Unauthorized Dan Brown Companion,* Citadel Press, 2006.

McDonnell , Shawn, *Preaching Another Jesus: Decoding Dan Brown's DaVinci Code Hoax,* Random House, 2006.

Rogak, Lisa, *The Man Behind the Da Vinci Code: An Unauthorized Biography of Dan Brown,* Andrews McMeel Publishing, 2005.

Shugarts, David A, Secrets *of the Widow's Son,* Orion, 2006.

Taylor, Greg, *The Guide to Dan Brown's 'The Solomon Key': The Essential Primer.* DeVorss & Company. 2005.

Zimmerman, W. Frederick, *The Solomon Key and Beyond: Unauthorized Dan Brown Update,* Nimble Books, 2005.

www.ingramcontent.com/pod-product-compliance
Lightning Source LLC
Chambersburg PA
CBHW060356090426
42734CB00011B/2153

* 9 7 8 1 6 0 8 8 8 0 1 1 9 *